D0850756

MUSIC AND MUSICIANS
IN VIENNA

MUSIC AND MUSICIANS
IN VIENNA

By Richard Rickett

GEORG PRACHNER VERLAG
IN WIEN

2. Edition 1981

ISBN 3-85367-019-9

©Copyright 1973
By Georg Prachner Verlag in Vienna
Cover design by Herbert Schiefer
Printed by Salzer - Ueberreuter in Vienna

CONTENTS

ACKNOWLEDGMENTS

---

*Photograph of the interior of the Vienna
Opera by courtesy of the Vienna State Opera.
Photographs of the Theater an der Wien,
Schubert playing the piano and the playbill
of the first night of Zauberflöte
by courtesy of the Archive of the
Austrian National Library.
Other photographs by courtesy of the
Gesellschaft der Musikfreunde in Vienna.*

The celebrated English conductor Sir Thomas Beecham once observed that a musicologist is a man who can read music but cannot hear it. And the Austrian writer Franz Grillparzer, a friend of both Beethoven and Schubert, opined that an analysis of music was like a description of a meal, course by course, mouthful by mouthful.

This is not to say that musicologists are not music-lovers, but it *is* to say that not all music-lovers are musicologists, and it is for music-lovers, beginners even, who would like to know a little more about Vienna's contribution to classical music that this book is intended. How many music-lovers realise, for instance, that virtually the whole corpus of what for convenience we call Viennese classical music was written within the span of forty-seven years, from 16 March 1781, when Mozart settled in Vienna, to 19 November 1828, the date of Franz Schubert's lamentably early death? And all this music was written in, or in the immediate vicinity of Vienna. Yet of the classical Viennese composers only one, Schubert, was actually born and bred in Vienna. What was it then that attracted other Austrian composers, not to mention Beethoven and Brahms from Germany, to settle in Vienna?

Perhaps Vienna's main attraction for a musician who had to make his way was that, in the eighteenth century at any rate, the Viennese aristocracy vied with each other in maintaining musical establishments ranging from a group of virtuoso performers to a private orchestra. If he was lucky and fell on his feet, as Gluck and Haydn did, a composer could be sure of a livelihood provided he toed the line (and this was where Mozart was ill-advised). A musician in the employment of one of the great Austrian or Hungarian families was as much part of the household as a footman, and was treated on the same level as a servant unless, like Haydn, he managed to charm his employer into recognition, however belated, of his international stature. Another factor of course was the fundamental Viennese addiction to music and the theatre: as a Burgtheater Director once put it: "If the theatre didn't exist, the Austrians would invent it." To make his mark in Vienna was the ultimate aspiration of almost every late eighteenth- and nineteenth-century composer.

A third inducement was the scope Vienna afforded a composer who was also a virtuoso performer. Here for once Haydn does not come into the reckoning, but both Mozart and Beethoven earned their daily bread in Vienna as pianists in the intervals of composing, only Beethoven had to give up owing to his deafness.

What this book particularly aims to stress is the *continuity* of Viennese classical music. The lives, and to some extent the works, of the two groups of composers that dominated Viennese music during the period under discussion were closely interwoven and frequently overlapped. The close friendship between Mozart and Haydn is common knowledge; Beethoven played for Mozart and later took lessons from Haydn, whom after an early tiff he venerated until the day of his death; Beethoven on his death-bed exclaimed that Schubert "had the divine spark in him"; and Schubert was a torch-bearer at Beethoven's funeral. Half a century later we find a warm friendship between Gustav Mahler und Hugo Wolf during their student days at the Vienna Conservatorium, and Mahler made no secret of the respect and affection he felt for Anton Bruckner, from whom he took some desultory and not particularly fruitful tuition.

Finally, the charge of superficiality has had to be incurred in the interests of keeping the book's weight down.

CHAPTER ONE

Christoph Willibald Gluck
1714–1787

Although Gluck's music is not often heard in Vienna nowadays he is an important figure in the history of Austrian music because it was he who paved the way for the Viennese classical composers by his drastic reforms in the domain of opera. As well as doing away with the absurdly stilted libretti on which Georg Friedrich Händel, for instance, wasted so much wonderful music, he insisted that opera must be first and foremost dramatic and not just a vehicle for vocal fireworks, for what Mozart called an "agile larynx". As a contemporary put it after seeing "Alceste": "It is nothing short of a miracle, an *opera seria* without castrati, singing without coloratura caterwauling, and an Italian libretto without pomposity or flattery."

Gluck first came to Vienna from his Franconian birthplace at the age of twenty-two, and after turning out his fair share of operas in the prevailing Italian style he settled in Vienna in 1751 and became private Kapellmeister to Prince von Sachsen-Hildburghausen, conducting the Prince's private orchestra at the Palais Rofrano, now Palais Auersperg. The summers were spent at Schlosshof in the Marchfeld (east of Vienna), where Gluck was presented to the Empress Maria Theresia in 1745. As time went on he established a fruitful partnership with the Court poet Pietro Metastasio, by common consent the foremost librettist of the day, and also wrote a number of French operas for the Court at a time when French culture was very much in vogue. In 1754 Maria Theresia, no doubt remembering him from the Schlosshof days, appointed him Kapellmeister to the Imperial Court. Among the "reformed" operas he produced during this period was "Orfeo" in October 1762, he himself conducting the first performance. "Orfeo" was also chosen for the ceremonies attending Joseph II's coronation as Holy Roman Emperor in Frankfurt on 3 April 1764.

Gluck's second "reformed" opera, "Alceste", appeared in 1767 and ran for over sixty performances. It was the success of his third "new" opera, "Paride ed Elena", in 1770 that finally consolidated Gluck's reforms and at long last dislodged the Italian faction from its hegemony, at any rate for the time being.

Gluck seems to have been a particular favourite with the Imperial family: at all events Marie-Antoinette, Maria Theresia's daughter and the new Queen of France, lost no time in summoning him to Paris as soon as she was installed there, and it was in Paris that he produced one of his finest works "Iphigénie en Tauride" (much admired by Schubert and Wagner) as well as a revised version of "Orfeo".

It was not until shortly before being awarded the coveted title of Court Composer in 1778 that Gluck returned to Vienna, wreathed in laurels and rolling in money. Basking in universal respect and esteem, he spent the last nine years of his life at his country house in what is now the Wiedner Hauptstrasse (just opposite the Carlton Hotel). Here he was visited more than once by Wolfgang Amadeus Mozart and his newly-wedded wife Constanze, and it was Gluck who used his influence with those in high places to secure a revival of Mozart's "Die Entführung" in August 1782. He further encouraged Mozart by personally attending a concert at which Mozart played one of his own Piano Concertos and conducted the "Paris" Symphony K 297, and by inviting the Mozarts to lunch afterwards. It was Gluck's proverbial hospitality that led to his sudden death at the age of seventy-three; not wishing to embarrass some guests by watching them drink while he abstained, he took a glass or two himself in defiance of his doctor's orders and paid the penalty.

It was Gluck who built the bridge from the Italian galant style to the operas of Mozart and to Weber's "Der Freischütz", which ushered in the German Romantic era; and his pioneer work was of immense importance to the full flowering of Austrian music, to say nothing of his resounding defeat of the Italian factions in Vienna and Paris.

CHAPTER TWO

Wolfgang Amadeus Mozart
1756–1791

Six years after Gluck settled in Vienna, Wolfgang Amadeus Mozart was born in Salzburg on 27 January 1756. The story of the early "infant prodigy" years is too familiar to need recounting in detail, and in any case does not fall within the scope of this book. His mother, Anna Maria, née Pertl, came from St. Gilgen, hence the charming statue near the Post Hotel in that delightful Salzkammergut town. His first teacher was his father Leopold, a musician in the service of the Prince-Archbishop of Salzburg. From his letters Leopold emerges as a rigid and humourless character with a good eye for capitalising on the phenomenal talents of Wolfgang and his sister Nannerl. Before he was five Wolfgang was being given elementary instruction in music by his conscientious father, though he probably had no need of it; at all events he was composing unaided before he was six. Small wonder then that father Leopold hastened to exploit this prodigy at the Courts of Vienna, Munich, Paris and London. On their first visit to Vienna in 1762 the Mozarts played at the Palais Colalto in Am Hof (still standing) next to the Church of the Nine Choirs of Angels, and it was after playing for the Imperial family at Schönbrunn Palace that Wolfgang clambered on to Marie-Antoinette's lap and announced that he had decided to marry her when he grew up (but without the formality of a proposal). Similarly, at the Paris Court he solemnly rebuked Madame de Pompadour for not kissing him. In London (1763) his success was only less sensational than Haydn's thirty years later. Father and son returned to Salzburg in 1766 before paying further visits to Vienna in 1767 and 1768, staying at what is now Wipplinger Strasse 25. Both visits brought abundant and fulsome promises but no concrete results whatever. In 1770 Wolfgang was appointed leader of the Prince-Archbishop of Salzburg's orchestra at the age of fourteen, but by now, after having spread his wings in Italy, the boy was beginning to realise that his drudgery as one of the Archbishop's servants was getting him nowhere, and as time went on he became increasingly restless in Salzburg, eventually developing a positively pathological aversion to Salzburg and all its inhabitants, whom he regarded as narrow-minded and uncouth. Nor did he enjoy being accommodated with the servants and treated like a lackey. But it was not for another three years that he managed to get leave from the Archbishop to visit Vienna. It was during this visit that he first met Joseph Haydn, and this was a turning-point in his life that must have confirmed his growing conviction that Vienna, not Salzburg, was where his destiny lay. Unfortunately however Vienna still failed to offer any prospect of a permanent post. So it was back to Salzburg again; but the very next year (1774) the eighteen-year-old Mozart managed to make his way to Munich, where he scored a resounding success with his opera "La finta giardiniera".

For all his dislike of Salzburg in general and of the new (1772) Prince-Archbishop Hieronymus Colloredo in particular, Mozart composed an immense mass of music during the next seven years. On his father's instructions he applied himself to the violin so that he could lead the small band at his disposal in the delightful Divertimenti and Serenades that he wrote for the Archbishop's Court or for important social occasions. The lovely "Haffner" Serenade (1776), for instance, was a wedding-present for Elisabeth Haffner, the daughter of the Mayor of Salzburg. Still, the rift with the Archbishop was widening all the time, and father Leopold was constantly on tenterhooks lest his son should finally kick over the traces and they would both find themselves out of work. So it was all to the good that Wolfgang was given leave in 1777 and set off for Paris with high hopes of securing a position there. As the Archbishop refused to release Leopold as well, Wolfgang was accompanied by his mother. The visit was a disaster; no offers were forthcoming, and Anna Maria died soon after they arrived in Paris.

A slightly less tragic disaster, but a disaster none the less, was Mozart's first serious love-affair: at Mannheim, much to his father's consternation, he fell in love with Aloysia Weber, a singer of sorts, and actually proposed to tour Italy with the entire Weber family, but fortunately this hare-brained project came to nothing because Wolfgang was ordered back to Salzburg forthwith, and by the time he was able to revisit Mannheim the Webers had moved to Munich. Mozart followed them, proposed, and was turned down, but consoled himself with a young cousin of his from Augsburg, a plain but spirited girl with whom he conducted a distinctly bawdy correspondence for a number of years.

And so to the fateful year 1781, when Mozart was twenty-five. At the start of the year he was in Munich putting the finishing touches to "Idomeneo" which was a great success in Munich but has never caught on in Vienna, largely owing to a somewhat static libretto and Vienna's congenital aversion to *opera seria*. After its first performance on 29 January Mozart was summoned by the Archbishop to attend on him at once in Vienna (Singerstrasse 7). By the time he arrived in Vienna Mozart was almost at the end of his tether as far as the Archbishop was concerned, and hardly a week went by without a letter to father Leopold asking for advice on how to extricate himself from the Archbishop's service. Leopold's concern can well be imagined: any more of this insubordination and his own as well as his son's employment would be in jeopardy. On

11 April Mozart wrote to his father that "even with only two pupils I am better off here than in Salzburg. But this inhuman villain will not allow me to accept outside engagements or give a concert". The crisis broke when the Archbishop gave him a personal dressing-down, accused him of laziness and disloyalty, and with what Mozart in a letter to his father called "all manner of *sottises* and *impertinences*" told him to pack his bags. The order was put into effect at the toe of a flunkey's boot, and the fact that it was a flunkey's and not the Archbishop's own august boot that delivered the final kick may well have seemed to Mozart the ultimate indignity, especially as in another letter to his father dated 17 March 1781 he had assured his parent that it was some consolation that he was at least being accorded the honour of being seated at table just above the cooks. What of course the flunkey could not know was that the boot that finally ejected Wolfgang Amadeus Mozart from the service of Hieronymus Colloredeo, Prince-Archbishop of Salzburg, kicked open the door to the Viennese Classical Era.

The intoxicating euphoria of his new freedom may serve to explain Mozart's immediate reaction: he went to live with the Weber family at what is now Tuchlauben 6, and wrote to his father on 15 December 1781 that he was in love with another member of this family, a sister of the Aloysia Weber who had turned him down a year or two previously. "Though not exactly ugly," he wrote, "she (Constanze) is far from beautiful. Her only real beauties are her pretty figure and her little black eyes. She has no wit, but enough common-sense for a wife and mother. It is a barefaced lie that she has no idea of money . . . She knows all about housekeeping and has the kindest heart in the world. I love her and she loves me with all her heart."

Love is indeed blind: other sources describe her as distinctly unattractive, and Mozart soon found that she had no more idea of money than he had.

In a letter to his sister dated 13 February 1782 Mozart describes his daily routine before he so unwisely surrendered his freedom: "My hair is always done by six in the morning, and by seven I have finished dressing. I then compose until nine. From nine till eleven I give lessons, then I have lunch unless I am invited to a household where they lunch at two or three. I can never start working again until five or six in the evening, and even then I am often prevented by a concert... If I get home early I compose a little before going to bed, sometimes until one in the morning."

But Constanze soon changed all that. She and Mozart were married on 4 August 1782 when he was twenty-six and she was barely out of her teens. Leopold's agitation can be imagined, and Constanze's mother was not very pleased either, as in order to be sure of getting Constanze to the altar Mozart had abducted her from her home and installed her in lodgings at what is now Graben 8. By a curious coincidence the bridegroom's present to the bride, so to speak, was the *Singspiel* "Die Entführung" (The Abduction), so there is a distinct autobiographical element in this enchanting work, especially as the heroine is named Constanze. It was first performed on 16 July 1782, i.e. about a fortnight before the wedding. Although it had been personally commissioned by Joseph II it very nearly foundered on the intrigues and machinations of the Italian clique under Antonio Salieri. Before long it was playing to packed houses all over Europe, and was particularly admired by the ageing Gluck, probably because it observed the spirit of Gluck's reforms in calling for singers who could act and actors who could sing. Yet despite the Emperor Joseph II's enthusiasm Mozart was still no nearer an official appointment with a guaranteed income, and in actual fact he earned very little from "Die Entführung", partly because there was no Performing Rights Society in those days, and partly because the composer of the music used to be billed in such small print that the casual reader would never even notice it.

On the whole however Mozart's prospects in Vienna were far from discouraging. He had plenty of pupils from influential families and was much in demand as a pianist, composer and conductor, so much so that he wrote to his father: "I assure you that Vienna is the finest place in the world for me to get on with my work." He was particularly successful with his Piano Concertos of which he wrote (again to his father): "They are a happy medium, not too easy and not too difficult; very brilliant, pleasing to the ear, natural, and sensibly written. There are occasional passages which only a professional musician will fully appreciate, but even these are so contrived that the layman will enjoy them too without quite knowing why." And of music in general he wrote: "Music must never offend the ear but always please it; in other words, it must never cease to be music."

For the first six months of his marriage Mozart was constantly on the look-out for an opportunity of presenting his beloved Constanze to his father in Salzburg, but for one reason or another—concerts and other commitments in Vienna, not to mention Constanze's apparently perpetual state of pregnancy—the visit was always being put off, and it was not until July 1783 that the journey to Salzburg was at last embarked upon. But relations with Leopold and Nannerl were far from cordial, and to add to the young couple's troubles came news from Vienna of the death of their first-born son Raimund, who had been born six weeks before his parents set out for Salzburg. During the birth Mozart had been utterly absorbed next door in the composition of the String Quartet in D minor K 421, the second of the set of six dedicated to Joseph Haydn. Of the Mozarts' six children, Raimund was one of the four who failed to survive infancy.

Even before Raimund's birth there occurred an incident, trifling in itself, which in retrospect is like Elijah's "little cloud the size of a man's hand on the horizon." In February 1783 Mozart wrote a "begging letter" to Baroness von Waldstädten asking for a loan to hold off an (unnamed) importunate creditor. Evidently Constanze's pregnancies and erratic housekeeping (for which she can hardly be blamed in the circumstances), coupled with Mozart's own fecklessness in money matters, were beginning to play havoc with the household budget. Still, the couple managed to move into more commodious premises at Schulerstrasse 8, and at the end of 1784 Mozart became a Freemason, whether or not at Gluck's instigation is uncertain. At all events, it was a step that apparently eased his conscience in the matter of writing begging letters. As for the move, it was only one of many; in their nine years of married life the Mozarts moved house ten times; a modest record by Beethoven's standards, but hardly a sign of stability.

The great event of 1785 was Leopold's return visit to Schulerstrasse 8 from February till April, during which a quartet consisting of Joseph Haydn (first violin), Ditters von Dittersdorf (second violin), Mozart (viola) and Johann Baptist Vanhall (cello) played for him some of the six quartets Mozart dedicated to Haydn. The room in which these historic gatherings took place can still be seen. The set of quartets was not completed until early the following year, but during Leopold's visit Haydn assured him that his son was "the greatest composer I know of either personally or by repute". During his stay Leopold also heard his son play in public a new Piano Concerto (in D minor, K 466), one of his very finest. The parts had only just been copied and Mozart played the solo part without even a preliminary run-through.

Along with Schubert's "Unfinished" symphony Mozart's mature operas are the most inexplicable phenomena in all music. There had been nothing remotely like them before, and there has been nothing like them since. They defy rational explanation. They also, nearly 200 years later, still fill opera houses all over the world. Yet by a cruel paradox it was "Le Nozze di Figaro", one of the most brillant of them all, that was the real cause of Mozart's decline and social eclipse. Three years previously, in 1783, a certain Lorenzo da Ponte, a writer and resourceful man of the world with influence at Court, promised Mozart to write a libretto for him as soon as he had discharged some tiresome commitments for the Court "Kammercompositeur" Antonio Salieri. Mozart had little trust in Italians, but da Ponte was as good as his word and in 1785 submitted a libretto based on Beaumarchais' comedy "Le mariage de Figaro". How da Ponte managed to get it past the censorship remains a mystery. At all events, in the course of a personal audience with Joseph II da Ponte succeeded in pulling wool over the Emperor's eyes by showing him excerpts in which the social satire had been considerably watered down, operating on the "what you mustn't say you can sing" principle. Mozart composed the music at what is now Graben No 8, and the first performance on 1 Mai 1786 was a tumultuous success, almost every number having to be repeated. Yet the intrigues of Salieri (who ironically enough had been a pupil of Mozart's friend Gluck) succeeded in getting it taken off after only nine performances. So Mozart took it to Prague, where it was an even greater success than in Vienna, himself conducting the first two performances. Encouraged by the warmth of his reception in Prague he also composed the lovely Symphony No 38 K 504 which he conducted the following January. Nor was the Symphony his only present to Prague, as we shall soon see.

Whether Mozart knew what he was doing when he allowed da Ponte to talk him into collaborating in such an out-and-out "anti-Establishment" opera as "Figaro" can only be conjectured. Not unnaturally, the Court and the aristocracy were "not amused" by the unconcealed satire on eighteenth century feudal rights and privileges, notably the notorious "jus primae noctis". They did not enjoy watching the master being outwitted by his servant. So what is probably Mozart's most universally popular Italian opera (and the first "modern" opera in the dramatic sense) cost him the loss of all his better-class pupils and shattered, at any rate for the time being, all his hopes of obtaining a well-paid post at Court. Even though the Emperor himself was by no means ill-disposed, from now on Mozart was ostracised from high society, and when in the last weeks of his life success came to him again, it was at a "suburban" theatre outside the pale. Worse still, Mozart was forced to resort to begging letters again, this time to a music publisher named Hoffmeister, offering him the sublime G minor Piano Quartet K 478 as security.

But if Vienna had turned sour there was always Prague, and it was in Prague that Mozart and da Ponte were to score their most spectacular success with "Don Giovanni" in the autumn of 1787. On the whole, Mozart must have reflected as he set out for Prague, it had been a year of violent ups and downs. First, there had been the occasion when the seventeen-year-old Beethoven, armed with a sheaf of enthusiastic "references" from influential personages in Bonn, presented himself and played to him. Mozart's verdict was: "This young man is worth watching; one day the world will acclaim his talent." What particularly struck Mozart was Beethoven's improvising rather than his actual piano-playing. Then in May there had come news from Salzburg of the sudden death of his father, and though relations between father and son had been distinctly strained since the marriage to Constanze, Mozart was bound to feel deeply the loss of one to whom he had always been able to turn for the advice and guidance he so sorely needed.

After some delay, "Don Giovanni" opened in Prague in the late autumn and was (in Mozart's own words) "a triumphant success". So much so that he was persuaded to try it out in Vienna too, but by now Vienna was no longer interested in Mozart, and it was given only fifteen times between May and December 1788. Even Beethoven criticised Mozart for wasting such noble music on such a frivolous libretto!

At the very end of 1787, at the age of thirty-one, Mozart was at last appointed Court Composer in succession to Gluck, but at less than half Gluck's salary, which drew from Mozart the comment: "Too much for what I do, too little for what I could do." And he never succeeded in securing the far better paid post of Court Kapellmeister. Among the first fruits of his new post was the Clarinet Quintet K 581, and later in 1788 came the magnificent triad of the last three symphonies 39, 40 and 41 written between June and mid-August, No 41 (the "Jupiter") being actually written in fifteen days! Yet all the while he and Constanze were signally failing to make ends meet in the household, largely because Constanze's ill-health was so expensive and she was constantly "taking the waters" at Baden, about twenty miles south of Vienna. The begging letters started again in June 1788, most of them directed to a brother Freemason named Michael Puchberg, who is assured of immortality through having come to the rescue so unfailingly. The letters contain all the usual protestations of "for the very last time", "as soon as my salary is paid", etc. etc.; and in one letter Mozart even offers pawn tickets as security. The valiant Puchberg was "touched" at regular intervals until 13 April 1791. There is also an isolated letter to Franz Hofdemel, another Freemason, dated March 1789. Hofdemel, too, duly "obliged".

Mozart never lived to hear any of the three great symphonies of 1788, and during the last three years of his life he wrote no more symphonies, as if leaving the field to his friend Haydn. Instead, he redoubled his efforts to regain a foothold in the Court Opera, but without success. Having temporarily exhausted the possibilities of Prague, and being demonstratively cold-shouldered in Vienna, where was he to turn? Shortly after his marriage he had seriously contemplated offering his services to England and had even started taking English lessons: "in three months I hope to be able to read and understand English books fairly easily". But father Leopold had put his foot down, and that was that.

Eventually, in the spring of 1789, Mozart was invited by Prince Lichnowsky to accompany him on a visit to Berlin via Prague, Dresden and Leipzig. He was politely received at the Prussian Court, but the only material result was a commission for six string quartets from King Friedrich Wilhelm II, who as an amateur cellist was very fond of chamber-music. In the event Mozart only completed three of them (K 575, K 589 and K 590), the latter being his last string quartet, and they were not published until after his death. So by July Mozart was back in Vienna, to find Constanze starting on another of her pregnancies. During this time the begging letters to Puchberg took on an even more desperate tone, but the autumn brought good news in the shape of a commission from Joseph II to write another opera; and "Così fan tutte", Mozart's third collaboration with da Ponte, was first performed on 26 January 1790.

From a purely musical point of view "Così fan tutte" is arguably Mozart's finest opera, but it has never enjoyed the universal popularity of the other four great operas, largely because its small proportions (only six characters) are unsuited to the vast open spaces of an opera house: it needs a more intimate environment. Sir Thomas Beecham once described it as "a long summer day spent in a cloudless land by a southern sea". From the very first, performances were clouded by the unexpected death of Joseph II, and once again a good deal of exception was taken to da Ponte's libretto, which was based on a notorious scandal that had rocked Viennese society to its foundations (an early but more elegant form of what is nowadays vulgarly known as "wife-swapping"). Richard Wagner of all people criticised the libretto's immorality, which he regarded as an insult to pure womanhood, as represented by Elsa, Elisabeth, Eva, Isolde and Co. It was due largely to the untiring efforts of conductors of the calibre of Gustav Mahler, Richard Strauss and Bruno Walter that "Così fan tutte" eventually took its rightful place among Mozart's supreme masterpieces.

As for da Ponte, he found it advisable to leave Vienna, and he settled in Trieste in 1792 before deciding to put the Atlantic Ocean between him and his "investigators". He arrived in the United States in 1804 after a forty-six-days voyage from London, and died in New York in 1838, aged eighty-nine.

Later in 1790 came what proved to be Mozart's last meeting with Haydn, who (with no Leopold Mozart to deter him) was embarking at the age of fifty-eight on his first visit to England. "Good-bye dear friend," said Mozart, "I have a feeling we shall not meet again." They never did.

Whereas Joseph II had never wavered in his support of Mozart, the new Emperor Leopold II was an out-and-out supporter of the Italian faction, and Mozart was still no nearer realising his hopes of a better-paid position at Court. Nevertheless, in a last despairing attempt to win the Emperor's favour he set off for Frankfurt to attend Leopold's coronation as Holy Roman Emperor, travelling via Nuremberg, which he describes in a letter as "a hideous town". He took with him the Piano Concerto in D (K 537) that is still known as the "Coronation Concerto", though whether he actually played it during the celebrations is uncertain, and its relative lack of inspiration suggests that his heart was not in it anyway. By the end of October he was back in Vienna with nothing to show for his pains, and no prospects of advancement at Court.

In the summer of 1791 a second son was born while Mozart was working on a new opera in German commissioned by a shrewd and resourceful impresario (and brother Freemason) named Emanuel Schikaneder, who also compiled the libretto. The opera was to be produced at the Freihaus Theater in what is now Vienna's Fourth District, i.e. well outside the city walls. Most of "Die Zauberflöte" was composed in a small summer-house in a garden near the theatre (the summer-house can now be seen on the premises of the Salzburg Mozarteum). The first performance was on 30 September, Mozart conducting the first two performances from the piano. After a somewhat slow start it packed the theatre night after night and was given no fewer than eighty-three times in a single year. On 7 October Mozart wrote to Constanze, who was doing one of her "cures" at Baden: "I have just come back from the opera, which was as full as ever ... You can see how this opera is becoming more and more popular." In another letter two days later he describes how he slipped behind the scenes one evening and played the Glockenspiel in Act I himself, much to the amusement of the cast, but not of Schikaneder, who was playing Papageno. Schikaneder also contributed some valuable suggestions about the music. It was he for instance who was really responsible for the "Pa-pa-pa-pa" duet between Papageno and Papagena. Mozart had written a fairly conventional duet, but at a rehearsal Schikaneder was not satisfied. "Mozart, this duet is not what I want at all: the music should express astonishment—first the two stare at each other in dumb amazement, then Papageno starts stammering 'Pa-pa-pa', Papagena does the same, until eventually they manage to blurt out each other's full name." Schikaneder also required a march during the assembly of the priests in Act II, and this Mozart is said to have supplied on the spot.

Within a matter of weeks Mozart was making money hand over fist. Written on the threshold of death, the music of "Die Zauberflöte" is arguably the purest, warmest and most sublime that even Mozart ever composed; nor is Schikaneder's libretto the farrago of nonsense it is often made out to be: if it had been, even Mozart's music would not have been able to invest it with immortality.

Just before completing "Die Zauberflöte" Mozart was interrupted by a commission to write an *opera seria* for the coronation of Leopold II as King of Bohemia in Prague. The subject chosen was "La clemenza di Tito" to an old libretto by the Court Poet Pietro Metastasio. Mozart dashed it off in three weeks, but any chance it ever had was dissipated by the royal party turning up an hour late and talking all through the first performance on 6 September. Yet on his return to Vienna Mozart conquered his weariness to the extent of writing the sublime Clarinet Concerto K 622. Another of his very last works was the profoundly moving "Ave verum". As for "La clemenza di Tito", it has had only two productions in Vienna this century, 1949 and 1976 at the Theater an der Wien, and it was given in the same years at the Salzburg Festival. It contains a great deal of music that only Mozart could have written, but the libretto is on the static side and it is a very difficult opera to produce, not to mention some fiendishly difficult arias.

About this time Mozart was visited at his last address, Rauhensteingasse 8, by a mysterious, sombrely-clad individual with a commission for a Requiem. In his state of almost total exhaustion Mozart became obsessed with the idea that the apparition was an emissary from the next world, and that the Requiem would in fact be for his own death (though he dated the manuscript 1792). Much romantic sentimentality has been lavished on the circumstances under which the Requiem was composed. There was in fact nothing at all supernatural about the commission: the "emissary" was merely the valet of a certain Count Walsegg-Stuppach who wanted to pass the work off as his own.

Be that as it may, Mozart became convinced that he was engaged on a race with death. Instead of completing each section of the Requiem before embarking on the next, he sketched out their opening bars only, so that in the event of his death they could be completed by another hand. One of his last actions as he lay dying was to puff out his cheeks in a despairing attempt to indicate how he wanted the trombones to sound in the "Benedictus". It is impossible to say with any certainty what was the very last music Mozart ever wrote, but it may well have been the "Lacrimosa". His last instructions before lapsing into a coma were to his favourite pupil Franz Süssmayr, and almost his last words were also to Süssmayr: "You see, I *have* been writing this Requiem for myself; I always told you so." With the help of another pupil named Joseph Eybler, Süssmayr arranged Mozart's fragments and sketches for public performance, and the work was first given in public at Wiener Neustadt almost exactly two years after Mozart's death. The view has sometimes been expressed that the work should never have been completed but preserved as Mozart left it, in which case one of his greatest masterpieces would have languished in a museum. Posterity should be grateful to Constanze for insisting that the work should be completed, even if her motives were primarily material: she needed the money.

What Mozart died of has been another favourite subject of speculation. In all probability it was sheer exhaustion that induced a kidney failure of some kind, though he himself was convinced he had been poisoned.

Constanze has been unjustly maligned for the circumstances of her husband's funeral. He was *not* buried in a mass grave, and that she did not accompany him on his last journey was probably due to the fact that she was too prostrated with grief to be able to face the appalling December weather. Although the house in Rauhensteingasse has recently been allowed to be acquired by a department store, the niche on the north-east wall of St. Stephen's Cathedral where Mozart's body was consecrated can still be seen. After that, it was conveyed to St. Marx Cemetery some way outside the city-walls: this too, though deconsecrated, can still be seen. But nobody could, or would, brave the elements all the way to the cemetery, and the few who started out soon turned back. Questioned later, the grave-digger did remember that the grave was somewhere near a lilac-bush . . .

Though so much is known about Mozart's daily life, his mental processes remain an eternal and supernatural mystery. Like Franz Schubert, he did not "compose" in the strict sense of the word: the ideas were already in his head when he sat down to commit them to paper, and unlike Beethoven he never made preliminary sketches or revisions. One might say he was born fully equipped. Hand him a violin, and he could play it: after hearing a piece of music once he could copy it out without a mistake. There is the famous story of the "Don Giovanni" overture being written in a few hours on the eve of the first performance in Prague, or of the March of the Priests in "Die Zauberflöte" being jotted down during a rehearsal. And after disposing of the manuscript of the Sinfonia Concertante K 297 b (Anhang 9), Mozart said it didn't matter because he could write it out again from memory.

Unlike Schubert, he was by no means reconciled to an early death, and complained that he had had "so little time to enjoy my talent". Yet in a letter to his father dated as early as 1787 he confessed: "I never go to bed without the thought that, young as I am, I may not live through the night."

In his short life Mozart wrote 626 works of all forms and sizes. Comparisons are odious, and whether or not Mozart was the greatest musician there has ever been is a matter of opinion. His music is an inimitable and unmistakable blend of exhilaration and gentle melancholy, which is why composers almost to a man have always venerated him as the supreme master, perhaps the most surprising verdict coming from Tchaikovsky, with whom Mozart would appear to have little in common: "Mozart is the culmination of all beauty in music . . . He alone can make me tremble with delight at the awareness of the approach of what we call the Ideal." In other words, has any composer ever given so much sheer delight, to use Tchaikovsky's word, to so many?

CHAPTER THREE

Joseph Haydn
1732–1809

All this time, down in the small town of Eisenstadt some thirty miles south of Vienna, Prince Nicolaus Esterházy's private Kapellmeister, Joseph Haydn by name, was diligently and conscientiously feeling his way, largely by trial and error, towards consolidating the structure of what eventually emerged as the classical symphony and string quartet. By trial and error, because as he himself said later: "Cut off from the outside world, and with nobody to divert me, I was forced to be original." He was forced to be prolific too, because his duties entailed producing music "on tap" for social occasions, birthdays, etc., and as his audience was to all intents and purposes identical from one week to the next he could never repeat himself: each successive work had to be different from its predecessor, and that with an orchestra of only twenty-four at his disposal. Haydn was composing before Mozart was born, yet it was not until after Mozart's death that virtually all his finest works were written. And by the time he died Beethoven had written six of his symphonies, and Schubert was a member of the Vienna Boys' Choir.

Joseph Haydn was born at the Lower Austrian village of Rohrau, about halfway between Vienna and Bratislava. The house where he was born is still well worth a visit, although it has unfortunately been very much over-restored. His father was a wheelwright and his mother a cook in the service of Count Harrach (the same family still maintains the local Schloss). In the year 1740 that saw the accession

31

of the Empress Maria Theresia he was taken on as a choir-boy at St. Stephen's Cathedral in Vienna, sharing with five other boys an exceedingly uncomfortable attic in a house (no longer standing) adjoining the Cathedral. When his voice broke in 1750 and he had to leave the choir, he moved into a tiny attic room in a house next door to the Michaeler Kirche, scratching a bare living by teaching and playing the organ at the lovely baroque church of the "Barmherzige Brüder" at Taborstrasse 16 in Vienna's Second District. He also earned a ducat or two from casual free-lance engagements to play at "Serenades" at noble mansions which he probably entered and left by the back door.

His first "steady" engagement as a professional musician was as a piano teacher to Countess Thun, who passed him on to Count Karl Joseph von Fürnberg, and this meant repeated invitations to spend the summers at the Fürnbergs' country seat, Schloss Weinzierl. It was in about 1757 that at the age of twenty-five Haydn fathered the classical string quartet by writing no fewer than eighteen of them for the Fürnberg family.

Having thus attracted the interest of the wealthier members of the aristocracy, Haydn was recommended in 1759 to Count Morzin, a Court Chamberlain, as being an ideal "personal Kapellmeister", i.e. a member of the Count's private household who could be relied upon to provide music as and when required. A menial post no doubt, but it gave Haydn the material security he needed, and above all it allowed him the leisure to compose during the summers at the Count's estate near Pilsen (now in Czechoslovakia). As well as being called upon, often at short notice, to supply music for social occasions—miniature operas, cantatas, divertimenti, and even Masses—he was also responsible for seeing that the musicians were decently turned out and discharged their duties to the Count's satisfaction. Unfor-

Wolfgang Amadeus Mozart

Joseph Haydn's birthplace at Rohrau in Lower Austria

tunately however Count Morzin's financial situation took a turn for the worse, and within only two years of Haydn's appointment the orchestra had to be disbanded, which was a particularly severe blow to Haydn because in 1760 he had fallen in love and married—but not the same girl. The girl he fell in love with felt constrained to enter a nunnery, whereupon Haydn, either from pure conscientiousness or because he couldn't be bothered to look any further (probably the former), proposed to her elder sister and was accepted. So both Haydn and Mozart married the sisters of their first loves, but in Haydn's case the marriage, like most marriages on the rebound, was a disastrous failure: she was extremely plain and uncommonly hot-tempered, and after four years of domestic discord they parted for good.

On the disbandment of Count Morzin's orchestra Haydn was soon snapped up by Prince Anton Esterházy, who was succeeded in 1762 by his brother Nicolaus, one of the wealthiest and most powerful noblemen in Hungary. Prince Nicolaus lost no time in appointing Haydn Deputy Kapellmeister at his palace at Eisenstadt (then in Hungary but now the capital of the Austrian Province of Burgenland) and here he remained for twenty-eight years, soon succeeding to the post of First Kapellmeister. Not content with the artistic splendours of his Eisenstadt palace, Prince Nicolaus built a second palace, complete with opera house à la Glyndebourne, at Esterház (now in Hungary) at the southern tip of Lake Neusiedl. Haydn wrote several Italian operas for Esterház before the opera house was almost totally destroyed by fire in 1779. What with one festivity and another the Prince became increasingly reluctant to say goodbye to the summer and return to Vienna, and as time went on Haydn's musicians became more and more irritated at being away from their Viennese homes until well into the autumn. Haydn championed their cause, and the result was the "Farewell" Symphony No 45, in the Finale of which the players leave the platform two by two until at last only two violins are left. The Prince took the hint.

During these twenty-eight years at Eisenstadt Haydn poured out an immense quantity of music, mainly symphonies and string quartets, but also some Italian operas for Esterház, which are seldom heard nowadays outside Austria. Notwithstanding the relative remoteness of Eisenstadt, the European aristocracy's grape-vine soon saw to it that the name of Haydn became a household word among the great patrician families: how else can one account for the fact that his "Seven Last Words of Our Saviour" (1785) was commissioned for the Good Friday service in the Cathedral of the far-off city of Cadiz? The "Seven Last Words" was described by Haydn himself as "a sequence of seven sonatas with an introduction and at the end an earthquake".

By the year 1781 that ushered in the Viennese classical era Haydn was regarded as the foremost composer in Europe and had been commissioned by the Court to write a set of string quartets, the so-called "Russian" quartets, for the State visit of the Grand Duke Paul of Russia. It may well be that it was these quartets that prompted Mozart to dedicate to Haydn the set of six quartets he wrote four years later.

Socially as well as musically, the twenty-eight years in the service of Prince Esterházy determined the pattern of Haydn's relations with the aristocracy. Though he started as a servant he was never a menial, and he handled his patron with a good deal more tact than Mozart showed in his dealings with the Prince-Archbishop. Haydn's contract stipulated that "he is to be treated and regarded as a member of the household". He "knew his place", but there was no inverted snobbery about him. If he was unpretentious, he was also far from servile. He was devoutly religious, and perhaps his outstanding trait was his extreme conscientiousness (as attested by his disastrous marriage). He was completely devoid of spite or malice, and not being involved as poor Mozart was in the hurly-burly of Court intrigues:

"Along the cool sequestered vale of life
He kept the noiseless tenor of his way."

But life at Eisenstadt and Esterház was too good to last: in 1790 Prince Nicolaus died, and his successor Prince Anton, convinced that the familiy fortune could be better spent than on the maintenance of a private orchestra, disbanded the players, Haydn included. So at the age of fifty-eight Haydn was free: that is, he had a pension but no patron (it was still the eighteenth century). The immediate necessity was to find somewhere to live, and he eventually moved into lodgings in Vienna on the site of Seilerstätte 15.

As one door shuts another opens: in far-off London an astute impresario named J. P. Salomon somehow got wind of Haydn being at a loose end and hurried to Vienna to try to lure him to London. Fortunately for Salomon, Haydn had himself been toying with the idea of seeing as much of the outside world as his friend Mozart had done, but he had been unable to decide in which direction to travel. Italy was an obvious choice, but Italy was too given over to opera, and Haydn, like Schubert, was not at his best when writing for the theatre, and wisely refused an invitation to write an opera for Prague after the overwhelming success there of Mozart's "Figaro" and "Don Giovanni". So Salomon's approach was well-timed: as well as offering very high fees for those days he commissioned six new symphonies and a number of lesser works.

Haydn was now fifty-eight and had hardly ever set foot

off the beaten track between Vienna and Eisenstadt. Yet he accepted Salomon's offer without the slightest qualms, and when his friends expressed their misgivings about his setting off for a far-off, draughty little island without even a word of English at his command he silenced them with an observation which in anyone else would have smacked of arrogance: "My language is understood all over the world." Just before leaving he enjoyed a day or two in Vienna with Mozart, who could not but blurt out his presentiment that they would never meet again.

Haydn's own account of the Channel crossing in a letter to his friend Marianne von Genzinger illustrates the outstanding traits of his character: "After hearing Mass I embarked at 7.30 a.m. and arrived at Dover safe and sound (for which thanks be to God) at 5 p.m. I stayed on deck the whole time in order to gaze my fill at that mighty monster the sea. As long as there was no wind I was not afraid, but when it began to blow hard and we were buffeted by huge waves I began to feel distinctly nervous and queasy. But I was not sick, though most of the other passengers were—they looked like death."

Haydn arrived in London on 1 January 1791 and with his natural courtesy and good humour soon had the capital at his feet. The wheelwright's son from Rohrau was entertained by royalty and feted with the kind of mass-hysteria nowadays engendered by public appearances of film stars or ski champions. In recognition of the award of his honorary Doctorate of Music at Oxford University his Symphony No 92 (the one dreaded by horn-players because of the octaves early in the Finale) became known as the "Oxford" Symphony; and the six symphonies commissioned by Salomon, Nos 93-98, included the "Surprise" Symphony with which Haydn deliberately startled a somewhat somnolent audience. The scoring of these first six "Salomon" symphonies shows how Haydn revelled in having a far larger orchestra at his disposal than he had ever handled before, especially in his writing for the percussion and the wood-winds in pairs.

During the first visit to London Haydn attended a mammoth Handel Festival in Westminister Abbey and was overwhelmed. "I realised I knew nothing and that I might just as well start all over again," he confessed.

Haydn set out on his return journey to Vienna in the summer of 1792, and on arrival acquired a house at what is now Haydngasse 19 in the Sixth District, though at that time it was still set amid unspoiled countryside. This remained his permanent address for the remaining seventeen years of his life, though he also kept on the pied-à-terre at Seilerstätte 15. Mozart was no more, but on the way back Haydn had stopped off at Bonn where a young pianist named Ludwig van Beethoven had been presented to him with a recommendation from Mozart, for whom he had played in Vienna five years previously. Haydn agreed to take him as a pupil at his Seilerstätte apartment in Vienna, and the lessons started in the autumn of the same year 1792, when Beethoven was twenty-two and Haydn sixty. From the very first it was an uneasy relationship, and although Haydn was one of the very few men for whom Beethoven entertained a sincere respect until his dying day, misunderstandings were inevitable in view of the difference in outlook and temperament between the two men. It was a clash of two centuries, the revolutionary spirit of the 1790s challenging the established order of the dying eighteenth century. Nowhere is the clash more vividly portrayed than in Beethoven's three Piano Trios Op 1, which Haydn refused to allow his unruly pupil to publish. Eventually Haydn was prepared to stretch a point in favour of the first two Trios, but drew the line at No 3, which Beethoven regarded as the best of the three. In the end Beethoven (inevitably) got his way and published all three.

Ever since Haydn's first conquest of London the irrepressible Salomon had been pressing for a return visit, and this Haydn embarked upon in January 1794. He is said to have toyed with the idea of inviting his pupil Beethoven to accompany him, but in the end he took with him as companion, copyist and personal valet a certain Elssler of Eisenstadt, whose other claim to fame is that he was the father of the celebrated dancer Fanny Elssler (1810-1884) who after touring all Europe also fascinated America. Socially, the second visit to London was as successful as the first: if there was less mass hysteria, there was an even more profound esteem. Musically, it added still further to Haydn's stature. Just how much it added can be gauged by comparing the first six "Salomon" symphonies 93-98 with the second set, 99-104; the sheer effervescence of their Finales is irresistible.

It was as a comparatively wealthy man that Haydn returned to Vienna in 1795. Punctilious and level-headed as ever, he had been a good deal more prudent in money matters than Mozart had been, nor had he ever allowed his head to be turned by universal adulation. To the end of his days he retained the innate courtesy that had earned the esteem and veneration of his contemporaries.

During Haydn's second visit to London Prince Anton Esterházy died, and his successor immediately set about reversing his predecessor's parsimonious economies. Haydn was retained on the Esterházy payroll as Honorary Chief Kapellmeister and was only required to reside at Eisenstadt during the summer months. It was not until these last years, perhaps in gratitude to Almighty God for the preservation of his creative powers, that after establishing the form of the classical symphony and string quartet he turned his attention to elaborating the scope of the Mass. Between 1796 and 1802, his seventieth year, he produced six superb Masses for performance in the Bergkirche at Eisenstadt on the name-day of the wife of his patron Prince Nicolaus II. The first of the six was the "Paukenmesse" of 1796, subtitled "Missa in tempore belli" because it was written at a time when Napoleon's troops had penetrated deep into Styria and were thrusting northwards; hence the prominence of the trumpets and drums (Pauken). The finest of the six, and arguably Haydn's finest work in any form (which is saying a lot) is the "Nelson" Mass in D minor, subtitled "Missa in angustiis", written in 1798 when Austria was indeed in dire straits ("angustiis") and Napoleon seemed to be carrying all before him. This time there are no fewer than three trumpets, one of which is given a solo part independent of the other two. The title "Nelson" is a reference to Nelson's victory at Aboukir on 3 August 1798 and to his official visit to England's ally Austria in 1800, during which Prince Nicolaus invited him to bring Lady Hamilton to Eisenstadt for a three-day visit. Haydn's D minor Mass was performed in honour of the occasion, and although Lady Hamilton seems to have had more of an ear for music than Nelson had, Nelson gallantly sat it through, and at a subsequent meeting with Haydn asked him for a souvenir, whereupon Haydn presented Nelson with the pen with which he had written the Mass. In return, Nelson gave Haydn the sword he had worn at Aboukir.

If Haydn's genius ripened slowly (nearly all his major works were written after he was forty) it also ripened steadily and came to its full flowering when he was over sixty. And if the "Nelson" Mass of 1798 is perhaps Haydn's finest work, the oratorio "The Creation" is certainly his most popular one. It represents the first fruits of the seed sown at the Handel Festival in Westminter Abbey seven years earlier, and the text based on Milton's "Paradise Lost" was originally intended for Handel. "The Creation" was first performed on 19 January 1799 at the old

Palais Schwarzenberg (Neuer Markt 8) and scored the kind of success that might have turned even Haydn's head. The massive choruses were something quite new in Viennese music, especially the famous C major outburst near the beginning "Und es ward Licht": its impact on the audience was comparable with that of the Hallelujah Chorus at a London performance of "The Messiah". As for the introduction, the "representation of chaos", it would not discredit a composer writing a century later. Vienna insisted on a sequel, and on 24 April 1801 "The Creation" was followed by "The Seasons" with another text from England based on Thompson's poem of the same name. In no other work is Haydn's affinity with his birthplace more pronounced, and it was in this year that he made a "sentimental journey" to the humble cottage at Rohrau where he was born, kissing the threshold before entering.

"The Seasons" left Haydn's creative powers exhausted. At the age of sixty-nine he professed himself "old and feeble, my strength is spent". His last active appearance in public was in 1803, and for the last six years of his life he was a legend in his own lifetime: his prudence in money matters enabled him to live comfortably, if not in luxury, at his home in Gumpendorf (Haydngasse 19) with the faithful Elssler to look after him. Yet although he was rarely seen in public his fame was more widespread than ever, and his two oratorios spread like wildfire all over Europe. His last public appearance was at a gala performance of "The Creation" in the Ceremonial Hall of the Old University (now the Academy of Sciences in Dr.-Ignaz-Seipel-Platz) on 27 March 1808. He was carried in by friends, and as he passed by even Beethoven bowed his head, which was not one of his more characteristic gestures.

Haydn was found dead in his bed on 31 May 1809, and Napoleon, who had occupied Vienna for the second time and had installed himself in Schönbrunn Palace, had a guard of honour mounted on Haydn's house and ordered his own grenadiers to fire a salvo of honour at the funeral. Haydn's body is interred in the Haydn-Mausoleum in the Bergkirche at Eisenstadt.

Joseph Haydn was the father of the classical symphony and string quartet, and laid down the lines on which Viennese church music was to be developed by Schubert and Bruckner, though Beethoven "deviated". As well as contributing to every known form of music Haydn invented a number of other forms hitherto unknown, and in the domain of oratorio he was the link between Handel and Mendelssohn.

But his own favourite composition was the melody of infinite simplicity and dignity that was to be the Austrian National Anthem from 1797 until 1918, and again from 1934 until Austria went under in 1938.

During his time in London Haydn had been immensely impressed by the dignity of "God save the King"; and in 1797, when Austria was being hard pressed by Napoleon's onslaught, he determined to write a "national hymn" for the birthday of the Emperor Franz. The house where this superb melody was born no longer exists, but it was on the site of the present Europa Hotel on the Neue Markt. The anthem was heard for the first time when the Emperor entered the royal box at the Vienna Burgtheater on the evening of his birthday, 22 February 1797. Copies of it had been distributed beforehand to the Provinces, so that the hymn could be played that same evening at National Theatres all over the Empire. For the rest of his days Haydn had a particular affection for his "Kaiserlied", and as soon as he was installed in his new house in Mariahilf he incorporated it in his String Quartet Op 76 No 3 which was first performed at Eisenstadt on 2 September of the same year.

When the Austrian Republic was reconstituted after the

Second World War the question arose of where to find a national anthem that would combine dignity with popularity and at the same time be essentially Austrian. From a nation-wide discussion in the Press three alternatives emerged:

1. To retain Haydn's anthem. There were of course considerable misgivings about its association with Nazi Germany, but on the other hand pleas for its restoration came pouring in from all sections of the population, from town and country alike, from people who felt that its simple dignity and emotional appeal had made it such an irreplaceable part of Austrian life that even the Nazi taint could be lived down.

2. To select some other melody from the rich storehouse of the Austrian classics and to announce a national competition for completely new words.

3. To announce a national competition for completely new music as well as words.

On 7 February 1946 a Committee from the Vienna Academy of Music reported unanimously in favour of the Haydn anthem, provided a suitable text was forthcoming; but on the following 12 March the Austrian Council of Ministers refused to approve the re-introduction of the Haydn anthem and instructed the Ministry of Education to invite suggestions for a new one, whereupon the Ministry duly organised a national competition for an anthem "with words and music in keeping with the character of the new Austrian Federal Republic". The response amounted to no fewer than 1,800 entries, so that it was not until 14 October 1946 that a melody alleged to be by Mozart was selected: a week later it was approved by the Council of Ministers. Whether the present anthem is really by Mozart is a vexed question. The melody is an appendix to Mozart's "Kleiner Freimaurer Cantata" written for the opening of a new branch of the "Zur neu gekrönten Hoffnung" lodge. The Cantata was one of his very last works, and Mozart himself conducted it on 18 November 1791 only a week or two before his death. In the original manuscript in the archives of the Vienna Gesellschaft der Musikfreunde there is no trace of the melody chosen for the new anthem, but a Cantata published by the Freemasons concerned a year after Mozart's death does include it. Stylistically as well as historically there is good reason to doubt its ascription to Mozart.

CHAPTER FOUR

Ludwig van Beethoven
1770–1827

In 1783 a certain Christian Gottlob Neefe, who was giving the thirteen-year-old Luwig van Beethoven piano lessons in Bonn, reported of his pupil: "This young genius deserves financial support to enable him to travel. He could certainly become a second Mozart if he goes on as he has started." It so happened that the Elector at Bonn at that time, Kurfürst Maximilian Franz, was a son of the Empress Maria Theresia, so there was no difficulty in despatching Beethoven to Vienna in 1787. On arrival, Beethoven lost no time in presenting himself to Mozart, who immediately recognised his outstanding proficiency: "This young man is worth watching: one day the world will acclaim his talent." However, any possibility of further contacts between the two was ruled out by Beethoven having to return to Bonn after only a fortnight owing to the serious illness of his mother, and it was not until five years later, i.e. after Mozart's death, that he returned to the Austrian capital armed with a sheaf of formidable introductions from personages in high places.

Though still intent on making a career as a pianist, Beethoven also took lessons in composition and counterpoint with Joseph Haydn, his object being to follow Haydn's example by securing himself an assured livelihood as personal pianist or Kapellmeister to one of the noble families who vied with each other in their patronage of music and musicians.

Haydn had already met Beethoven in Bonn on his way back from his first visit to London, and had promised to accept him as a pupil in Vienna. But the sixty-year-old Haydn and the twenty-two-year-old Beethoven did not always see eye to eye on musical matters, and the lessons were discontinued after a disagreement over Beethoven's Piano Trios Op 1. However, Beethoven had already fallen in love with Vienna (and not only with the scenery), and for the remaining thirty-five years of his life Vienna was his home. The recommendations from Bonn opened all doors to the local aristocracy, and it was greatly to the credit of the Viennese upper classes that they treated Beethoven with respect, and accorded him the social standing that he felt was his due. Their tolerance of such an inordinately sensitive and testy character with strong republican sympathies and a habit of repaying kindness with the most appalling rudeness was a vital factor in Beethoven's decision to settle in Vienna for good. As Carl Czerny, one of his pupils, put it: "One wonders whether he would have been tolerated so patiently in any other country in the world. In Vienna he was always regarded as something out of the ordinary, and even people who failed to understand him were instinctively aware of his greatness."

Between Beethoven and Haydn there was no ill-feeling whatever; on the contrary, Haydn reported to the Elector at Bonn: "Beethoven will *in time* become one of the greatest musicians in Europe, and I shall be proud of having been able to call myself his teacher."

It was as a pianist that Beethoven originally made a name for himself. He made his first public appearance in 1795, when he was twenty-five, and soon established himself as the most powerful pianist in Vienna. But by the time he wrote to a friend of his in Bonn "I am getting on well, better every day", it was not only as a pianist that he was attracting attention. He had smartened himself up, and was even something of a social lion; and by the end of the eighteenth century he was well launched on his career as a composer, with the Piano Sonatas up to Op 22 in B flat (i.e. including the "Pathétique"), the first three Piano Concertos, and the first set of String Quartets (Op 18) to his credit.

It was at the age of twenty-eight that Beethoven first began to suspect that his hearing was not all it should be. For a time he refused to believe that the affliction was anything but temporary, but by the time he completed his First Symphony in 1800 he was forced to contemplate the possibility of chronic deafness, and by 1801 he realised that there could be no cure. In 1802, in an access of utter despair, he gave vent to the agonised "de profundis" known as the "Heiligenstädter Testament" because he was living at the time at Probusgasse 6 in the outlying village of Heiligenstadt:

> "O you people who hold me to be hostile, obstinate and misanthropic, how greatly you wrong me! You do not know the secret cause of that which gives you this impression. From childhood upwards my heart and my spirit were inspired by gentle feelings of kindness, but only consider that for six years I have been affected by an incurable condition . . . Born with a fiery and lively temperament, and very susceptible to social pleasures, I was early forced to segregate myself and to spend my life in solitude. What humiliation when someone is standing near me and hears a far-off flute and I cannot hear a sound! Or when someone hears a shepherd singing and I can hear nothing! Such experiences nearly drove me to despair, and it would have taken little to make me end my life: one thing alone, the art of music, restrained me."

But it was not until 1804 that he had to be shouted at, and as late as 1809 he complained of the noise of Napoleon's bombardment of Vienna and moved into a basement in Rauhensteingasse (near the house in which Mozart died) in order to get away from it. But in 1808 he had to give up appearing in public as a pianist, and in 1812 he began to withdraw from society. Yet in December of the following year he was still able to conduct the first performance of the Seventh Symphony, and in 1814 he directed the first performance of the final version of "Fidelio" at the Kärntnertor Theater, hoping against hope that a visit to Teplitz to "take the waters" the year before might effect some improvement, if only temporarily. But after 1818, when he was forty-eight, any kind of normal conversation was out of the question; all remarks had to be submitted in writing, and the "conversation notebooks" that have been preserved are perhaps even more poignant than the "Heiligenstädter Testament".

But although he fought off the almost suicidal depression of the "Heiligenstädter Testament" Beethoven was far from satisfied with his work: "henceforth", he wrote, "I intend to tread entirely new paths". Hence that memorable evening of 14 August 1804 when at Prince Lobkowitz' mansion (within a stone's throw of the Hotel Sacher) an invited audience heard the first (private) performance of the Third Symphony ("Eroica") and were no doubt shocked and bewildered by the dissonances in the first movement, which in those days must have sounded like grinding discords. No wonder that the first public performance at the Theater an der Wien on 7 April 1805, Beethoven himself conducting, was cooly received. But Beethoven had kept his promise: the "Eroica" is indeed an "entirely new path", and represents the watershed between the eighteenth-century elegance of Mozart and Haydn and the revolutionary ardour of the Napoleonic era.

Notwithstanding the patronage of great noblemen such as Prince Lichnowsky, Prince Lobkowitz and Prince Rasumovsky, the French Revolution sounded the deathknell of private orchestras and "personal" virtuosi. Nineteenth-century music belonged to the middle-classes, and Beethoven's world was as different from Haydn's as Schubert's was from Beethoven's.

Unlike Mozart and Schubert, Beethoven composed laboriously and revised meticulously, particularly in the case of his only opera "Fidelio", over which he spent nine years. The first performance of "Leonora", as it was originally entitled, was at the Theater an der Wien on 20 November 1805, i.e. during the first French occupation of Vienna, the audience being mainly composed of French officers who were hardly likely to be in sympathy with the opera's glorification of liberty. Small wonder then that it dropped out of the repertoire after only two months. Undaunted, Beethoven set about tautening up the libretto, but the revised version, also at the Theater an der Wien in 1806, fared little better than the first. Mindful perhaps of Mozart's experience of the fickleness of Vienna's taste in opera, Beethoven next toyed with the idea of getting "Leonora" put on in Prague, but only got as far as writing yet another overture, the "Leonora No 1" of 1807, and the Prague performance never materialised. It was not until 1814 that a second revised version which involved "Leonora" changing her name to "Fidelio" scored a triumphant success at the venerable Kärntnertor Theater, the overture on this occasion being the one now known as the "Fidelio" Overture. It was Gustav Mahler who while Director of the Vienna Opera initiated the present practice of playing the magnificent "Leonora No 3" Overture as an entracte in Act II.

In the summer of 1806 Beethoven went to stay with his friend Count Brunsvick in Hungary in order to escape from the irritations of the French occupation of Vienna, and during his stay he fancied himself "engaged" to his host's sister Theresa. Hence the exuberant high spirits of the Fourth Symphony, with its "perpetuum mobile" Finale and a slow

Ludwig van Beethoven
A portrait in the possession of the Gesellschaft der Musikfreunde

Schubert at the piano (1826) with Bauernfeld, Kupelwieser, Schwind, the Fröhlich sisters, Vogel and Grillparzer

movement that was particularly admired by Hector Berlioz. Nothing of course came of the "engagement", though years later Beethoven dedicated to Theresa one of the loveliest of his Piano Sonatas, the Op 78 in F sharp major which is known to have been one of his own favourites. Theresa was only one of a number of blue-blooded young ladies to whom Beethoven became attached at one time or another, but his eccentric and often uncouth behaviour was an insurmountable barrier to the domestic happiness he so desperately longed for. Behind his disconcerting exterior was a fundamentally affectionate disposition, as is evidenced by the devotion he lavished on his worthless nephew Karl; but though highly susceptible to feminine charms he had no understanding of women whatever, and in his later years he came to realise how utterly he had also failed to understand life in general, largely because (except as a musician) he was to all intents and purposes uneducated.

About the Violin Concerto, first performed at the Theater an der Wien in December 1806, a contemporary "critic" wrote: "Opinions differ on the merits of Beethoven's Concerto, and despite some passages of real beauty there is a lack of cohesion about it, and the endless repetition of a few commonplace themes soon becomes tedious". No comment.

The next four symphonies appeared in pairs, the Fifth and Sixth (Pastorale) in 1808, and the Seventh and Eighth in 1812. The easy-going Fourth Symphony had come as a surprise after the rugged grandeur of the "Eroica", but the Fifth restored the balance with a vengeance. It was first performed in December 1808 at a concert at the Theater an der Wien organised by Beethoven himself, the programme also including the Sixth Symphony, the Fourth Piano Concerto, the Choral Fantasia, and a number of lesser works. Contemporary accounts give no information about what proportion of the audience actually sat all this out to the bitter end (the adjective bitter also applied to the temperature of the theatre), though a visitor to Vienna who had managed to secure tickets wrote: "The ninth item on the programme was a large-scale symphony, much too long. A gentleman sitting next to us remarked that he had had a look at the parts on the cello desks during a rehearsal, and they ran to thirty-four double sheets. Note-spinners in Vienna seem to be as long-winded as lawyers." Presumably the unknown visitor was too cold, tired or bored to notice that Beethoven's Fifth is the first symphony to use trombones and the first to run the third and fourth movements together.

Beethoven was the first subjective composer, and the most subjective of all his works are the Fifth and Sixth Symphonies, especially the latter. It is the expression, in Beethoven's own language, of his reaction to the natural beauties of the Viennese countryside, the villages (not yet suburbs) of Heiligenstadt, Nussdorf, Döbling, Grinzing and Sievering to the north-west of the city, at the foot of the vine-clad slopes on which he loved to wander for hours on end. "Nobody can love this countryside more than I do," he wrote to Baroness Theresa Malfatti, and it may well be that the beauty of the landscape, especially of the Vienna Woods, was one of the factors that induced him to settle in Vienna in the first place. In later life it almost certainly compensated for, or at any rate mitigated, the appalling affliction of his total deafness. Writing in 1823, his friend and biographer Anton Schindler describes a walk in the lovely Wiesental between Heiligenstadt and Grinzing: "Beethoven stopped and surveyed the landscape with a look of ecstasy in his eyes; then sitting down on the grass with his back against an elm tree he asked whether there was a yellow-hammer singing in its topmost branches. There was no yellow-hammer. Then he said: 'This is where I composed the scene by the brook (the second movement of the Pastoral

Symphony), and the yellow-hammers and quails, the night-ingales and cuckoos all round me played their parts.'" But one wonders whether, by the time he was working on the Pastoral Symphony, Beethoven was able to hear bird-song at all. The aura of the Vienna countryside "played its part" in a good many other compositions too. Parts of "Leo-nora", for instance, were composed in the woods stretching up to the Gloriette in Schönbrunn Park, while most of the Ninth Symphony was written at Baden bei Wien. Mödling was another favourite haunt in his later years. Which is why, notwithstanding all the stately mansions he frequented and the innumerable town houses he lodged at, he so often turned his back on the city and strode out beyond the glacis into the countryside; and why Beethoven himself termed the "Pastoral" Symphony "more an expression of a feeling for Nature than a depiction of natural beauty".

By March 1809, the year after the Fifth and Sixth Symphonies, it was apparent that Haydn's strength was ebbing (he died on 31 May), and in view of Vienna's prestige as the capital of music it was deemed advisable in high places to take steps to ensure that Beethoven remained in the Austrian capital, particularly as in the previous year Napoleon's brother Jérome had offered him a post at the Westphalian Court. Accordingly a group of noblemen headed by the Archduke Rudolf (the youngest son of the late Emperor Leopold II), Prince Kinsky and Prince Lobkowitz jointly sponsored a scheme whereby he was assured an annuity on condition that he remained permanently domiciled in the Emperor's domains. With the assistance of a legal friend Beethoven had a document drawn up confirming the settlement and professing that "he derives so much pleasure from his residence in the capital, is so full of gratitude for the many demonstrations of goodwill that he has been vouch-safed, and is such a patriotic admirer of the country in which he has settled, that he will always be proud to regard

himself as one of the goodly company of Austrian artists".
Unfortunately the annuity subsequently involved Beethoven
in a lot of tiresome litigation as most of it evaporated in the
great inflation brought about by the interminable Napoleonic wars. But Beethoven kept his side of the agreement,
the furthest he ever found himself from Vienna being when
he was "taking the waters" at Teplitz.

The most important work of 1810 was the Fifth ("Emperor") Piano Concerto.

The next pair of symphonies, the Seventh and Eighth,
made their appearance when the episode with Theresa von
Brunsvick was at an end and Beethoven was consoling himself with Goethe's friend Bettina von Brentano. The Seventh Symphony has been subjected to almost as many fan-
ciful interpretations as the Fifth. The house in which he
wrote it looked directly on to the glacis on which Napoleon's cavalry used to exercise, so it is perhaps not too
far-fetched to detect an allusion to the cantering of horses
in its Scherzo. The Eighth is the most exuberant, and certainly the most Viennese, of Beethoven's symphonies, and
as usual with Beethoven its high spirits are in startling contrast to the circumstances under which it was composed. He
had been to Teplitz in the hope that the waters would miti-
gate his deafness, and the horns of the post-chaise are a
prominent feature of the Trio, while the last movement is a
musical joke: bowling irrepressibly along in F major it is
suddenly disrupted by a terrible C sharp, and it is only after
a series of desperate modulations that the movement eventually rights itself. On his way back from Teplitz Beethoven
stopped off at Linz and had a flaming row with his younger
brother Johann, who was teetering on the verge of an inju-
dicious marriage—the same Johann who once signed himself in a letter to his brother Ludwig "Johann van Beethoven, landowner", to which Beethoven returned an answer
signed "Ludwig van Beethoven, brainowner".

The Congress of Vienna in 1814 was an ideal opportunity for the Austrian capital to parade Beethoven for the admiration of all Europe. At a marathon concert in the Redoutensaal of the Hofburg on 29 November 1814 the Seventh Symphony shared the honours with two somewhat mediocre works, one a cantata entitled "Der glorreiche Augenblick" (The glorious moment), and the other a piece of symphonic proportions called "Wellington's victory at Vitoria" with an "all-star" cast; Beethoven conducting, Antonio Salieri manipulating the cannonades, Johann Nepomuk Hummel playing the drums, and Giacomo Meyerbeer working the thunder-machine.

The Eighth Symphony was followed by the last five Piano Sonatas (the last of all, Op 111, being dated 1822), and the Missa Solemnis (1818–1823) commissioned by the Archduke Rudolf, the youngest son of Leopold II, who in 1819 was consecrated Prince Archbishop of Olmütz (now in Czechoslovakia). Next came the last six string quartets that reach out to the uttermost limits of this particular form, and even of tonality itself.

Ever since about 1817 Beethoven had been turning over the idea of setting Friedrich Schiller's "Ode to Joy" to music, but it was not until 1824 that the early sketches, after exhaustive polishing and refurbishing, were eventually incorporated into the Finale of the Ninth Symphony, which was completed at Baden and first performed at the Kärntnertor Theater on 7 May 1824. It was twelve years since Vienna had heard a new symphony by Beethoven, nor of course had it heard, or even heard of, Schubert's "Unfinished" Symphony which was actually composed two years before Beethoven's Ninth. The final transactions involving the sale of the Ninth Symphony reflect the precarious state of Beethoven's finances at the time. The Ninth Symphony was originally commissioned by the Royal Philharmonic Society of London, who had paid Beethoven £50 for it in

1822; yet it was not until 25 March 1825 that the symphony was performed in London after Beethoven had offered it to four different publishers.

A visitor described Beethoven's circumstances in 1825, two years before his death: "Beethoven invited me to sit down, and himself sat down on a chair by the bed and pulled it up a yard or two to a table covered with manuscripts he was working on at the time. I cast a quick glance round the room: it had two windows and was about the same size as the vestibule. By one of the windows was a piano, apart from which there was not the slightest suggestion of decent comfort, let alone luxury. A desk, a table and two chairs, white walls with faded, dusty hangings—that was all. So there I was sitting next to this morose, ailing sufferer. His bushy hair was almost completely grey, and his face seemed smaller than portraits of him had led me to expect ... His skin was brownish, but not with the healthy kind of tan that comes from an open-air life; on the contrary, there was a streak of yellow in it. His nose was narrow and pointed, his mouth generous, his pale grey eyes small but eloquent. His expression was a blend of pensive melancholy, suffering and goodness, without a trace of the inflexible determination of his iron will ..."

It was no doubt his rapidly deteriorating health that prompted his bitter outburst: "You people of Vienna don't want real music any more: Rossini and Co are your heroes, and you are no longer interested in Beethoven ... It's Rossini, Rossini all the time."

In the last months of his life Beethoven's sight was impaired as well as his hearing, and he also suffered from a disorder of the liver. But in the end it was pneumonia that carried him off, and characteristically he died in the middle of a thunderstorm (in March!). How much the Viennese regarded him as one of themselves was demonstrated at his funeral: from the house where he died in Schwarzspanier

Strasse (just behind the Votivkirche) to the Alser church is about 1,000 yards, yet the cortège took over an hour and a half to cover the distance. In his funeral oration Austria's leading poet and dramatist, Franz Grillparzer, affirmed his belief in Beethoven's immortality: "While bidding farewell to the mortal who is no more, we are left with the heritage of a mind that is still with us and always will be." Behind the coffin walked all the most prominent figures in the artistic life of Vienna, and one of the torch-bearers was Franz Schubert . . .

Whereas most of the houses associated with Mozart have disappeared, many of Beethoven's are still standing; but tracing Beethoven's endless changes of address in Vienna is about as complicated an exercise as trying to unravel the story of "Il Trovatore". Quarrels with landlords, and notices to quit for rampageous behaviour were almost everyday occurrences. What with his irascibility and his habit of playing the piano at all hours, not to mention his "singing", his neighbours must have moved as often as he did. Furthermore, especially when he was engrossed in a new work, Beethoven demanded a standard of accommodation that was by no means easily come by in the Vienna of those days. The view from his window had to be extensive and picturesque, and the room itself had to be large and sparsely furnished so as to allow him plenty of room to pace up and down. Another habit of his was to litter the floor with scraps of musical inspiration that kept flashing across his brain. At one time or another he lived at no fewer than twenty-five different houses within the city's boundaries, fourteen of them in the Inner City.

Two years after settling in Vienna, Beethoven was ensconced in a house belonging to Prince Karl Lichnowsky in what is now the Alser Strasse (Ninth District), and it was here that he composed the three Piano Trios of Op 1 that led to his difference of opinion with Haydn. In 1795 he was lodging at a house on the corner of Löwelstrasse and Metastasiogasse, almost next to the present Burgtheater, and in 1799 and 1800 he was at Tiefer Graben 10. The Second Symphony was written at Probusgasse 6 in Heiligenstadt, which has been preserved exactly as it was then. It was also at this house that he poured out his soul in the "Heiligenstädter Testament".

In 1803 Beethoven undertook to write an opera for the Theater an der Wien and was given permission to take up residence in the theatre itself, where he remained until 1806. Simultaneously he had rooms of his own at Mölkerbastei 8, opposite the present University, as well as summer country quarters at what is now Döblinger Hauptstrasse 92, where he composed the "Eroica" Symphony and parts of "Leonora". The summer of 1808 was spent at what is now Grinzinger Strasse 64, a typically suburban house in Empire style which is still standing. Only a narrow passage separated his rooms from the summer quarters of the Grillparzer family, the young writer being then seventeen years old. One day Beethoven caught Grillparzer's mother listening at the keyhole while he was playing the piano: he at once stormed out of the house and never played there again.

In 1809, aged thirty-nine, he was living at a house in Schreyvogelgasse between Teinfaltstrasse and the Dr.-Karl-Lueger-Ring, and from 1810–1814 he returned to Mölkerbastei 8, where he composed the "Emperor" Concerto and the Seventh and Eighth Symphonies. By 1817 however he was showing a marked preference for country life, first at Landstrasser Hauptstrasse 26, and in May and June at Pfarrplatz 2 in Heiligenstadt (still preserved). 1818–1820 were passed at Mödling: 1818 and 1819 at Hauptstrasse 79, and 1820 at Achsenauergasse 6, where Beethoven composed parts of the "Missa Solemnis". The following winter he returned to the district Landstrasse before moving first to Unter Döbling and then to Baden, Rathausgasse 10. On 3 October 1822 he returned to Vienna to go through the motions of conducting the Overture "Die Weihe des Hauses" Op 124 for the re-opening of the renovated Theater in der Josefstadt, lodging at what is today Laimgrubengasse 22 (Sixth District).

In the spring of 1823 Beethoven was the guest of Count Pronay at what is now Hetzendorfer Strasse 75a before returning to Baden (Rathausgasse), where he completed the Ninth Symphony and warmly welcomed a visit from Carl Maria von Weber. In the autumn he returned to Vienna, first to Ungargasse 5 (still standing) in the Third District, and in 1824 to Hadikgasse 62 in Hietzing; and it was at these addresses that he wrote his last string quartets. The summer of 1824 he spent at Schloss Guttenbrunn at Baden, and in autumn 1825 he moved to Schwarzspanier Strasse 15, where he remained until his death on 26 March 1827 at the age of fifty-six.

CHAPTER FIVE

Franz Schubert
1797–1828

After Beethoven's funeral Schubert and one or two of his closest friends repaired to an inn "Zur Mehlgrube" on the Neue Markt and Schubert proposed a toast to "him we have just escorted to his grave". A moment or two later he proposed a second toast to "him that will be the next". Eighteen months later Schubert himself was dead, at the age of thirty-one.

Of all the great composers none has been more grotesquely misrepresented than Schubert. One authority calculated not so long ago that there have been 896 films (and goodness knows how many novelettes, etc. of nauseating sentimentality) presenting Schubert as an easy-going suburban bumpkin of inconceivable naivety who in female company could only stammer and blush; an idler who sponged on his friends, who spent his mornings turning out romantic songs with mechanical regularity, and his afternoons roaming the Vienna Woods with his head full of waltzes before settling down with some cronies to booze away until the small hours at some picturesque "olde worlde" tavern in Grinzing. Not to mention the unspeakable musical "Lilac Time", of which Richard Strauss observed that its perpetrators ought to be locked up. On the other hand, it would of course be even more misleading to go to the other extreme and depict Schubert as at best a layabout and at worst a hippie with no fixed abode.

Yet if misrepresented after his death, during his brief lifetime Schubert was hardly represented at all. Outside a

small circle of kindred spirits he was almost completely unknown, let alone understood. The one public concert of
his music did not take place until he had only seven
months to live, and brought him in "the princely sum of
800 gulden" (about £ 30). The misrepresentation of Schubert is understandable only in so far as his true nature is
still a baffling enigma. Even his closest associates were often puzzled by the apparent inconsistency of his behaviour. Although he was convivial enough in the company of
his intimate friends he was ill at ease in formal society and
avoided social gatherings whenever possible. It was only at
rare intervals that a kindred spirit was vouchsafed a
glimpse of the spiritual conflict behind his unremarkable
exterior.

Of all the great Viennese composers Schubert was one
of the few who was actually born and bred in Vienna. He
was born on 31 January 1797 at Nussdorfer Strasse 54—
the house is now a museum but has been over-restored
and "tidied up". At the time Schubert was born Goethe
was forty-eight and Schiller thirty-eight: Mozart had been
dead six years, Haydn was working on "The Creation",
and Beethoven, already a remarkable pianist, was on the
threshold of his tempestuous career as a composer. Schubert's father was a schoolmaster and Franz was the twelfth
child, but eight of his brothers and sisters died before he
was two years old, and the only member of the family
with whom he was on terms of lifelong intimacy was his
brother Ferdinand, who was three years older than himself. At the age of eleven young Franz was sent to the
"Konvikt" in Dr.-Ignaz-Seipel-Platz, next to the Jesuit
Church, a boarding-school run by Piarist monks which
served as a choir-school for the Chapel Royal (Vienna
Boys' Choir). Here he was given a free education until
1813 but did not enjoy the strict regimentation, though he
did enjoy the singing and playing in the orchestra, of

which he eventually became the leader. It was here, too, that he met Josef von Spaun, who secretly procured Schubert the vast quantities of music-paper he consumed without his father finding out, and who was to prove his truest lifelong friend without ever really understanding the workings of Schubert's creative mind.

On leaving the "Konvikt" at the age of sixteen Schubert was liable to conscription into the army, a fate he only averted by allowing himself to be conscripted into his father's school, where he taught the bottom form, ages five to six, in return for board and lodging and precious little else. One cannot imagine that Franz would have made a very good soldier, with his short sight and diminutive stature (five feet two inches). Notwithstanding the soul-destroying drudgery of teaching the three R's at elementary level he found time to compose his first symphony and his first Mass. But his precocity was tempered with diffidence: "In my heart of hearts," he confessed to Spaun, "I should like to amount to something, but who can hope to achieve anything after Beethoven?" It was many years before Schubert succeeded in throwing off this inferiority complex vis-à-vis Beethoven, and the common heresy of judging Schubert by Beethoven's standards still persists. Although the two composers died in successive years Schubert's world was totally different from Beethoven's, and his finest works are those that are tinged with a romanticism quite alien to Beethoven. In other words, Beethoven was not Schubert's only contemporary: the arch-romantic Carl Maria von Weber loomed equally large, and Schubert represents the almost imperceptible transition from the classical to the romantic era. Thus on 19 October 1814, at the age of seventeen and while still teaching at his father's school, he laid the foundation-stone of the German Lied with the wonderful "Gretchen am Spinnrade", followed shortly by the even more romantic "Erlkönig".

Even before Schubert left the "Konvikt" Salieri, the Court Composer who had concocted so many intrigues against Mozart, tried to persuade him to give up the idea of Lieder and concentrate on Italian opera, yet of Schubert's dozen or so essays in writing for the theatre none are performed nowadays except the incidental music to "Rosamunde". Until his dying day Schubert was tantalised by an unrequited love for the theatre, and on one occasion he even sold his school-books to buy a ticket for "Fidelio". His own failure to write a successful opera was the most grievous of his many disappointments, the nearest he ever came to success being a piece called "Die Zauberharfe" that ran for twelve performances at the Kärntnertor Theater.

Schubert's eighteenth year, 1815, was one of the most miraculous in his pitifully short life. Brahms once observed that the amount of music Schubert poured out in that single year was enough to make other composers give up in despair: 144 Lieder, including the "Erlkönig"; two Masses; the Second and Third Symphonies; two Piano Sonatas and a number of smaller piano pieces; and a string quartet written in seven days. And all this in the intervals of teaching! Spaun wrote: "Mayrhofer and I went to see Schubert at his father's school (now Säulengasse 3 in the Ninth District) and found him pacing up and down in a sort of ecstasy reading Goethe's poem 'Der Erlkönig' aloud. Suddenly he sat down and started writing, and in no time at all this marvellous song was committed to paper. As Schubert had no piano we rushed round to the 'Konvikt', where it aroused the greatest enthusiasm." So much so that Spaun wrote a flowery and pompous letter to Goethe enclosing forty-four settings by Schubert. Goethe never even deigned to answer. Spaun next sent a copy of "Der Erlkönig" to the publishers Breitkopf and Härtel of Leipzig, who duly contacted the only Franz Schubert they knew, an elderly and pedantic note-spinner at the Dresden Court who testily enquired in return who this impertinent bungler was who was sullying his good name with such rubbish.

Later that same year Schubert fell seriously in love for the first and last time in his life. Six years later he confessed to his "friend" Anselm Hüttenbrenner: "There was one I loved dearly and she loved me too. She was the solo soprano in one of my Masses and sang sublimely and with great feeling. She was not at all pretty, in fact her face was pock-marked, but she was good and kind through and through. For three years we hoped to get married, but I was unable to secure a position that would give us enough to live on. So in the end she fell in with her father's wishes and married someone else, much to my sorrow. I still love her dearly and there has never been anyone I loved so much since. I suppose she was just not meant for me." The girl in question was Theresa Grob, the daughter of a local soap manufacturer, and the "someone else" was a master baker.

From time to time Schubert indulged, or was involved, in encounters with the opposite sex, but he was not, and never attempted to be, attractive to women. Anselm Hüttenbrenner described him as "short, round-faced and rather tubby. He had a low forehead, a snub nose, and thick, bushy hair. He was short-sighted and always wore glasses, even in bed. He dressed in whatever came to hand and usually smelt of pipe-tobacco. He disliked having to spruce himself up, which was why he never attended gatherings of people he did not know. He did not look attractive or even intelligent: it was only when playing or composing that his whole expression changed and there was a fascinating, even demoniac look about him. As a pianist he was far from elegant, but he was accurate and competent and a wonderful accompanist of his own Lieder. His stubby fingers could even manage his most difficult sonatas. He was also extremely quick at reading from score."

In his reminiscences, the writer Eduard Bauernfeld, another of Schubert's friends, stresses the duality of Schubert's nature, the alternation of typically Viennese light-heartedness with periods of profound melancholy. His unsociability was due not so much to shyness as to a realisation that as he moved in a world that others could not comprehend, it was better to keep himself to himself than to expect people to understand it. A certain Pauline Grabner, who was still living in Graz in 1903, aged ninety-two, could remember him as "unaffected and natural, subject to fits of depression but very sociable among his own friends. He was on the corpulent side and rather careless about his dress. He always spoke Viennese dialect."

Without the circle of intimate friends who supported him after he had left his father's school because he could no longer endure the drudgery of teaching, Schubert's short life would probably have been even shorter. As well as taking it in turns to house him and ensure that he did not starve, they were all kindred spirits, creative and original. The first of them, Josef von Spaun, was the most sensible and practical of them, but it was the more volatile Franz Schober who came closest to penetrating Schubert's innermost world, and it was to Schober that Schubert wrote his last despairing letter on his death-bed. The most intellectual of the circle was Johann Mayrhofer: Schubert frequently lodged at his house at Wipplingerstrasse 2 and set over forty of his poems to music. Apart from Schober, Schubert was happiest in the company of Moritz von Schwind and Leopold Kupelwieser, two painters who were among the last to join the circle. Schwind, who was seven years younger than Schubert, owned a house near the Karlskirche with a lovely garden, full of lilac and acacia, that inspired some of Schubert's finest Lieder, including "Hark, hark the lark".

The only one of the circle who was not young was Michael Vogl, a singer at the Opera who came to know Schubert and his Lieder through Schober. Vogl was also a friend of Mozart's pupil Süssmayr, and being thirty years older than Schubert and already celebrated he at first adopted a somewhat condescending attitude towards a composer of whom few people had even heard; but after being induced to run through some of Schubert's settings of poems by Mayrhofer, with Schubert himself at the piano, he championed Schubert to the extent of taking him on extended tours of Salzburg and Upper Austria, and used all his influence to propagate Schubert's Lieder in the aristocratic circles to which Schubert himself had no access.

Schubert and his friends used to foregather at regular intervals for "Schubertiades", meetings of kindred spirits united by common interests and enthusiasms. Poetry readings and discussions alternated with Vogl singing Schubert's latest Lieder, after which there would be dancing, with the wives joining in. If Schober, Schwind and Kupelwieser were the mainstays of these gatherings, Schubert himself was the central figure, though he seldom left the piano and never joined in the dancing or the more robust activities which followed. He was also extremely wary of forming new acquaintanceships, creative ability being his sole criterion. Before agreeing to meet a stranger he would enquire "Kann er was?", "Is he any good at anything?", a habit that earned him the nickname of "Canevas".

A casual visitor to a Schubertiade wrote: "We went to a hearty Schubertiade at Spaun's. The painter Kupelwieser was there with his wife, and so were Grillparzer, Schober, Schwind, Mayrhofer, Gahy (who played some marvellous piano duets with Schubert) and Vogl, who sang about thirty glorious Lieder ... After the music there was plenty to eat, and then the dancing started. Shortly after midnight

Franz Schubert and the singer Michael Vogel
A drawing by Franz Schober

Johann Strauss II

we adjourned to the 'Grüner Anker' in Grünangergasse and had the time of our lives." Bauernfeld gives a similar account in his reminiscences: "At our Schubertiades there was good company, gallons of wine, the admirable Vogl giving a superb account of Schubert's Lieder, and Franz himself having his work cut out to force his stubby little fingers to do justice to the accompaniments. For the dancing, when we were joined by our wives, poor Franz was exploited even more outrageously: he had to keep playing his latest waltzes until he was positively bathed in perspiration, and it was not until we sat down to supper that he was allowed a breather." Sometimes however Schubert used to disappoint his friends by not turning up, and would excuse himself next day by saying he just hadn't felt in the the mood.

As well as the "Grüner Anker", other small-hour haunts were the "Ungarische Krone" and Bogner's coffee-house at the corner of Blutgasse and Singerstrasse.

Who paid? According to Bauernfeld: "Usually two of us had no money, and the third had none at all. Occasionally Schubert sold a song or two, but the money never lasted long." Whenever they could afford it, Schubert and his friends would make expeditions into the Vienna Woods and sometimes even further afield, one of their favourite haunts being the Schloss at Atzenbrugg, near Tulln, which was administered by a relative of Schober's. In the summer there would be country-dancing and in the winter snow-balling, from both of which Schubert held aloof. From what has survived of Schubert's diary it is clear that he shared Beethoven's love of the Viennese countryside. There is also an entry dated 14 June 1816: "As if from afar comes the magical sound of Mozart's music. O Mozart, immortal Mozart, how many countless imprints of a better life have you implanted in us!"

After taking the drastic step of walking out of his father's school Schubert had no fixed abode apart from two summers in Hungary in 1818 and 1824. For the time being he sought refuge at Schober's in Landskrongasse, and the firmness of his resolve to devote himself henceforth to music and music alone is manifested in his highly uncharacteristic outburst: "The State owes me a living, I was put into the world to compose."

Like so many other Viennese, Schubert was bowled over by Gioacchino Rossini, whose operas were taking Vienna by storm as early as 1816, though he did not appear in Vienna in person until six years later. Unlike Beethoven, and later Wagner, Schubert found Rossini, especially "The Barber of Seville", delightful, and "could not deny that he has extraordinary genius", but he also prophesied that the Rossini craze would soon evaporate, which it did. As if to compensate for his disappointment at being unable to write a successful opera himself Schubert produced three more symphonies in quick succession, the Fourth (Tragic) and the delightful Fifth in 1816, and the markedly Italianate Sixth in the winter of 1817–1818. The Fifth was actually performed once in his lifetime, but the Fourth had to wait until twenty-one years after his death, and the Sixth was rejected by the Vienna Philharmonic in the last year of his life.

Anselm Hüttenbrenner described Schubert's routine at this time: "Schubert would seat himself at a desk at 6 a.m. and compose without a break until close on 1 p.m., only breaking off to fill his pipe. Whenever I visited him he would play over what he had written if there was a piano available, and ask me what I thought. He never worked in the afternoon: after lunch he would make off into the country, or to a coffee-house, where he would order a black coffee, smoke a pipe, and read the papers. In the evenings he would usually manage to get into a theatre."

Schubert's two summers in Hungary were the only occasions he ever travelled beyond the frontiers of even the shrunken Austria of today. One of his friends secured him a temporary post as music teacher to the two daughters of Count Johann Karl Esterházy at the princely salary of the equivalent of 10p an hour, plus free board and lodging at the Count's castle at Zselesz (now in Czechoslovakia, north of Budapest and east of Bratislava). Socially Schubert was still diffident and ill at ease in his pupils' company, though with the servants he was less inhibited: "The cook is rather skittish," he wrote to Schober on 8 September 1818, "but the rest of the staff are all very nice. The housemaid is very pretty and I see quite a lot of her. The Count is rather uncouth and the Countess somewhat haughty. The two girls are nice children. So far I have been spared the ordeal of eating with the family . . . My quarters are comfortable and there is a lovely garden, but the geese, about forty of them, make such a noise you can hardly hear yourself speak." In all probability it was the pretty housemaid, Pepi Pöckelhofer, who was the cause of the disease that hastened Schubert's premature death. For the time being however the long, hot Hungarian summer did his health a world of good, and he had time and an agreeable environment for composing.

The following summer he embarked upon the first of his tours with Vogl, starting at Kremsmünster in Upper Austria and going on to Steyr, still one of the most beautiful market towns in Central Europe. Here Schubert was accommodated by a local music-lover who had eight daughters, all pretty: "Never a dull moment," Schubert wrote to his brother Ferdinand. After visiting Linz, Schubert and Vogl returned to Vienna by Danube steamer, and back in Vienna Schubert completed the "Trout" Quintet that he had started on at Steyr. So one of his most mature and lovable chamber-music masterpieces was written at the tender age of twenty-two: needless to say it was never publicly performed during his lifetime.

The most important work of 1812 was a Symphony in E which he sketched in full but never orchestrated. The original manuscript has had an interesting career: eighteen years after Schubert's death his brother Ferdinand gave it to Felix Mendelssohn, who declined to orchestrate it. Twenty-four years later Mendelssohn's brother Paul gave it to Sir George Grove (much to Brahms' indignation), and it is now in the library of the Royal College of Music in London. In 1934 the sketches were orchestrated by the conductor Felix von Weingartner, and it is this version which is sometimes given today. The existence of this symphony raises the question of the numbering of Schubert's symphonies, about which there has always been considerable confusion. In all probability Schubert wrote ten symphonies, not nine. The first six are correctly numbered: No 7 is this sketch in E major, and No 8 is the "Unfinished" of 1822. No 9 is perhaps the "Gastein" symphony of 1825: Schubert presented it to the Vienna Gesellschaft der Musikfreunde in October 1826, and the manuscript has never been seen since. The "Great" C major Symphony of 1828 would therefore be No 10, not 9. There is however a school of thought that maintains that the "Gastein" and the "Great" C major are one and the same symphony, the latter being a revised version of the former.

The remarkable thing about the "Unfinished" Symphony is not that it consists of only two movements but that it was written as early as 1822, two years before Beethoven's Ninth. The "Unfinished" Symphony, like Mozart's operas, is a phenomenon of which there is no rational explanation, especially when one remembers that Schubert was only twenty-five when he wrote it. Most of it was composed when he was living with Schober at Spiegelgasse 9 in the First District. The original manuscript had an even more remarkable history than that of the E major Symphony. Two years after stopping work on it Schubert sent it to

Anselm Hüttenbrenner, the Director of the Styrian Music Society, in return for having been elected to honorary membership of that body. Though claiming to be one of Schubert's closest friends Hüttenbrenner never performed a single work of Schubert's during his period in office, and true to form he sat on the manuscript of the "Unfinished" for over forty years, perhaps hoping one day to pass it off as his own. In 1865 however Johann Herbeck, Court Kapellmeister in Vienna, visited Hüttenbrenner near Graz to see if he could recommend any new works for performance in Vienna. Hüttenbrenner grudgingly opened a drawer full of old manuscripts, among them the "Unfinished". After laboriously wheedling it out of Hüttenbrenner's clutches Herbeck and the Vienna Philharmonic performed this miraculous work for the first time on 17 December 1865, thirty-seven years after Schubert's death.

By 1823 the Schubertiades were beginning to lose their original exuberance: Kupelwieser was in Rome, and Schober had been attracted to Breslau in the hope of making a career on the stage. By August Schubert was in a state of abject depression, aggravated by his failure to obtain a foothold in the Vienna Opera owing to the phenomenal success of Rossini, and also by a serious illness which meant a stay of several weeks in hospital (Allgemeines Krankenhaus) during which he wrote the first half of the song-cycle "Die schöne Müllerin" to poems by a German romantic poet named Wilhelm Müller. A return visit to Steyr with Vogl in the early autumn speeded his convalescence, but in an affectionate, almost emotional letter to Schober he wrote: "Although I am a good deal better I am beginning to wonder whether I shall ever be really well again. I am leading a very simple life, enjoying plenty of walks and reading Walter Scott ... Vogl is a good travelling companion, and he sang very well in Linz and Steyr."

December 1823 was notable for the first performance of "Rosamunde" at the Theater an der Wien, the book being by the egregious Frau von Chezy who with her inept libretti had been the ruin of Weber's "Euryanthe" and was now the ruin of "Rosamunde". Schubert's incidental music to this ill-starred piece was among the Schubert manuscripts so dramatically discovered by Arthur Sullivan in 1867 in the archives of the Vienna Gesellschaft der Musikfreunde, where the dust-covered package had been languishing for over forty years.

By January 1824 Schubert was definitely in better shape, thanks to less irregular habits and a strict diet. He found the atmosphere at Schwind's house stimulating and congenial, and walks with Schwind in the Vienna Woods were benefiting him physically. Mentally however he was still at a low ebb. "No one can really know another's joys and sorrows," he wrote in his diary. "People fondly imagine they can communicate with one another, whereas in reality they are poles apart, and this is indeed a melancholy reflection." And in a letter to Kupelwieser in Rome he wrote: "Every night I go to bed I hope I may not wake ... Imagine a man whose health will never again be what it was, whose inspiration is flagging and whose fairest hopes have been dashed; a man to whom love and affection bring nothing but pain ... and ask yourself whether you can conceive of anybody so utterly wretched. Every new dawn is a repetition of yesterday's unhappiness. The one bright spot in my monotonous existence is Schwind, whose company brings back memories of the old days ... Instead of Lieder I am trying my hand at instrumental music, feeling my way towards a full-scale symphony. The latest news from Vienna is that Beethoven is giving a concert including his new symphony (the Ninth), three extracts from a new Mass (the Missa Solemnis), and a new Overture. Pray God I may one day give a concert of this kind." He did, but not until 26 March 1928 (the anniversary of Beethoven's death) when he had only another seven months to live.

One of the "instrumental works" was the A minor String Quartet, with a second movement "borrowed" from the "Rosamunde" music; and it was actually published in the autumn of the same year. His "feeling my way towards a full-scale symphony" took the form of the Octet, first performed at the house of the amateur clarinet-player who commissioned it, stipulating that it was to be as much like Beethoven's Septet as possible. No sign here of "flagging inspiration", yet this wonderful work was only performed once more before its rediscovery in 1861.

In May 1824 Schubert embarked upon a second summer at Zselesz and is generally supposed to have come very close indeed to falling in love with his pupil Caroline Esterházy, by now seventeen. According to some accounts she archly reproached him one day for never having dedicated anything to her, whereupon Schubert stammered: "It's all for you anyway." As on his previous visit he ate with the servants and was only the hired music teacher, but this time he did at least have a room of his own, and once again the Hungarian summer did his health a power of good; but long before the time came to return to Vienna he was missing his friends terribly. "There is no intelligent conversation here", he wrote.

Bauernfeld describes the sort of life Schubert was leading with Schwind and Schober in 1825: "We often used to stroll around till the small hours before turning in at the house of whichever one of us was prepared to put us up. We were not particular about furniture, etc., and Schwind usually slept on the floor wrapped in a leather coat. Clothes were common property. Whichever of us happened to have any money did the paying, and it was Schubert who from time to time lorded it over us like a Croesus after managing to sell a song or two. One day, for instance, the publishers Artaria paid him 500 gulden (about £ 18) for some of his Walter Scott Lieder. But the money was soon gone and then we were back where we started."

In June 1825 Schubert plucked up the courage to write to Goethe (this time in his own hand) enclosing some of his settings, among them "An Mignon", "Ganymed", and "An Schwager Kronos"; but as in 1815 Goethe did not even condescend to reply, though there is an entry in his diary: "26 June 1825. From *Schubart* in Vienna a parcel of *my* Lieder (sic!)".

In mid-May Schubert set out with Vogl on another tour of Upper Austria and Salzburg and lodged at Steyr with the same bevy of females as in 1819. He also spent six very happy weeks in Gmunden, where he started on the lost "Gastein" symphony and composed several Lieder to poems by Sir Walter Scott. In July he and Vogl visited Linz and St Florian before returning to Steyr and thence to Gastein, a three days' journey from Steyr in those days. During August and September they were in Salzburg, where Schubert was astonished to find grass growing in the streets and all the great palaces and mansions silent and deserted following Napoleon's suppression of the Archbishopric in 1803. But he was captivated by the view from the Nonnberg and particularly admired St Peter's Abbey. On his return to Vienna the Schubertiades were revived with something of the former ebullience, but by the end of the year Schubert was again prostrated by blinding headaches and was not at the usual "grand New Year's Eve" Schubertiade. Yet it was at this nadir of his material and spiritual fortunes that he completed his last two (and finest) String Quartets, the D minor ("Death and the Maiden") over which he spent two years, and the G major written in ten days in June! Writing over forty years later, Ludwig Speidel relates how one day Schubert submitted the "Death and the Maiden" Quartet to the famous Schuppanzigh Quartet who specialised in Beethoven's quartets. They started to play it through, but after all sorts of mishaps gave up halfway through the first movement, Schuppanzigh declaring that it was unplayable and not the proper way to write a quartet anyhow; whereupon Schubert just smiled, collected up the parts, and went on his way without a word.

Schubert was one of a group of musicians who visited Beethoven eight days before his death on 26 March 1827. Hearing that Schubert was waiting outside, Beethoven ordered his amanuesis to show him in first: he had come across some of Schubert's Lieder and piano duets and had been moved to declare "this Schubert certainly has the divine spark in him". The same year saw the final dissolution of the Schubertiades, mainly because Schwind had emigrated to Munich and Schubert himself was again being tormented by fits of depression and agonising headaches. Yet between February and October he wrote the first fourteen Lieder of the "Winterreise" song-cycle, setting of more poems by Wilhelm Müller that are among the most deeply-moving of all Schubert's works. When he sang them through at Schober's house in Landskrongasse where he was then lodging, Schober having abandoned his theatrical venture in Breslau, Schubert's friends found them unbearably gloomy, and Schober confessed that the only song he liked was the "Lindenbaum". "Personally I like them more than any of my other Lieder," Schubert insisted, "and one day you will too."

Two other fine works written in the year Beethoven died are the two Piano Trios in B flat and E flat. The former was performed privately at Spaun's the following year, and the latter was not only performed at the public concert of Schubert's works on 26 March 1828 but was actually published in Leipzig just before his death. These two

Trios, the last two String Quartets, and the "Winterreise" are sufficient proof that Schubert had at last emerged from Beethoven's shadows; and when he visited Graz in September he must have hoped for some support from his "friend", the specious Anselm Hüttenbrenner, who as Director of the Stryian Music Society was surely in a position to further Schubert's cause. But the "Unfinished" Symphony still languished in the bottom drawer of Hüttenbrenner's desk.

And so to 1828, the last year of Schubert's life and arguably one of the most important years in the history of Western music; a year in which Schubert poured out a stream of masterpieces that point the way ahead to Anton Bruckner forty years later. It also saw the first and only public concert of his works, a venture that brought him in the equivalent of £ 30, with which he paid off some debts and bought a piano. There was no time now for tours of Upper Austria or Styria, or even for occasional outings with Schober: his only relaxation was a journey with his brother Ferdinand to Eisenstadt, where he stood awhile in silence by Haydn's tomb. The first fruits of this miraculous year was the great C major Symphony, completed in March, which suffered the usual fate of Schubert's later symphonies. He first offered it to the Musikverein, who rejected it as "too big and too difficult". The Vienna Orchestra tried to play it through but could not, or would not, go through with it, so Schubert presented the orchestra with the "little" C major, No 6, instead. The manuscript of the "great" C major then disappeared until it was unearthed by Robert Schumann on 1 January 1839 during his visit to Vienna to go through some music in the possession of Ferdinand Schubert. Schumann promptly sent it off to Leipzig, where it was performed at the Gewandhaus the same year, Mendelssohn conducting. Indeed, Mendelssohn was so enthusiastic about it that he put it down for a Royal Philharmonic concert in London in 1844, but the orchestra emulated their Viennese colleagues by refusing to exert themselves beyond the first movement. It was not until December 1839 that the first two movements (!) were performed in Vienna, and it was another eleven years before the symphony was performed in its entirety in Vienna. Schumann waxed lyrical over its "heavenly length, music one could listen to for ever". "This symphony," he went on, "transports us into a world where we cannot recall ever having been before." The conductor Hans von Bülow used a similar metaphor: "We are transported into eternal regions, into a world without time."

Next came the profoundly moving Mass in E flat (June and July), a predominantly choral work in which the soloists have little scope apart from the remarkable. "Et incarnatus est", which is a duet for two tenors. The Kyrie is almost indistinguishable from Bruckner's early church music. It is hardly necessary to add that Schubert never lived to hear it. It was followed (August-September) by the C major String Quintet with two cellos: curiously enough Schubert makes no reference in his correspondence to this supreme masterpiece, which is why virtually nothing is known of the circumstances of its composition; it was not even published until 1853.

Schubert's Piano Sonatas, after a century and a half of neglect (Sergei Rachmaninov for instance never even knew they existed until shortly before his death) are now being taken up by pianists all over the world. Of all Schubert's works, the Piano Sonatas have suffered most by being compared with Beethoven's, whereas in point of fact they are much more closely akin to Weber's: their form is loose and their mood is essentially lyrical. Schubert's last three Piano Sonatas were written in three weeks of September, the last of all being the sublime Sonata in B flat (D 960).

Appropriately enough, Schubert's last work was a group

of songs posthumously entitled "Schwanengesang" (Swansong), "Die Taubenpost" being the last song he ever wrote. By this time he was suffering frequent attacks of giddiness, and in September he left Schober's house on doctor's orders and moved into lodgings outside the city walls on the banks of the river Wien (now Kettenbrückengasse 6 in the Fourth District) where it was hoped that the country air would do him good, though he himself was loath to move because he was afraid nobody would come so far out of town to see him. The neighbourhood of the river Wien was far from salubrious, and the house, being new, was damp. Schubert had always been irresponsible where his health was concerned, and in a matter of weeks his already enfeebled constitution was an easy prey to typhoid fever. His last letter, addressed to Schober, is preserved in the tiny room which was Schubert's last dwelling:

12 November 1828.

"I am ill. For eleven days I have eaten nothing and drunk hardly anything, tottering back and forth between my chair and my bed . . .If I do manage to force something down I immediately bring it all up again. Seeing that I am in such a wretched condition, do please try to find me something to read. I have been reading Fennimore Cooper, including 'The last of the Mohicans', so if you can lay your hands on anything else of his, please leave it at Bogner's coffee-house (Singerstrasse), where my brother can be relied upon to collect it for me. Or some other book . . ."

For a time he was still able to sit up in bed correcting the proofs of the "Winterreise", but then he lapsed into delirium: "Why isn't Beethoven here?" Then turning his face to the wall he murmured: "This is the end of me", and he died at 3 p.m. on 19 November 1828, aged thirty-one. His doctor gave the cause of death as "nervous fever" which in all probability meant typhoid fever, possibly aggravated by syphilis. His last wish to be buried next to Beethoven in the Währing Cemetery in Währingerstrasse was carried out on 22 November, though his body now rests in the Musicians' Corner of the Central Cemetery.

In his "Neue Musikalische Zeitschrift" Robert Schumann wrote in 1838 of Schubert's "everlasting youth", and a day or two after Schubert's death Schwind wrote to Schober: "The memory of him will stay with us, and all the disorders of this mortal life will never dim our recollection of what it was that has gone from us for ever . . . The more fully I comprehend what he was, the more clearly I realise what he must have suffered."

Schubert died at an age when Beethoven had just put the finishing touches to his First Symphony, yet in the eleven years which were all he had to devote himself exclusively to composition he produced seven Masses; over eighty smaller choral works; ten symphonies; eleven overtures; 450 piano works; over thirty chamber-music works: and over 600 Lieder! The Deutsch catalogue of his works runs to over 960 items. The only branch of music he left untouched was the Concerto. His pre-eminence as a composer of Lieder has tended to obscure his instrumental works, yet there are times and moods when only one of the last quartets or the C major Quintet will satisfy. And has he not also left us two of the most sublime syphonies ever written?

No tribute could be more appropriate than the epitaph by Austria's leading dramatist Franz Grillparzer:

"Music has here etombed a rich treasure but still fairer hopes."

The original grave on which this epitaph is inscribed can be seen in the "Schubert Park" in der Währinger Strasse, the now deconsecrated cemetery in which Schubert was buried alongside Beethoven. Later, the bodies were moved to their present graves in the Central Cemetery.

CHAPTER SIX

The Viennese Waltz and Viennese Operetta
Johann Strauss I and II

With the death of Schubert the forty-seven years of what we call the Viennese Classical Era came to an end. The musical hegemony of Europe passed for the time being to the Romantics—Weber, Schumann, Mendelssohn, Berlioz, and Liszt—while Vienna was bemused by the lighter fare served up by Johann Strauss I and Joseph Lanner, whose lilting marches, waltzes and polkas assuaged the passions that had been inflamed by the bitter operatic conflict between the German Romantics, represented by Carl Maria von Weber, and the Italian invasion led by Rossini. The dance music purveyed by Strauss and Lanner was also a predictable manifestation of the long period of peace maintained by the Metternich regime after the turmoil of the Napoleonic wars, though the origins of the waltz can be traced back to long before the turn of the century. The Trio of Mozart's String Quintet in C major (K 515) for instance is a waltz in all but name, and in the opera "La cosa rara" (1787), by Mozart's contemporary Soler, a couple actually danced a waltz on the stage. Mozart's interest in this opera can be presumed from the fact that he quoted from it in "Don Giovanni".

In many people's minds the waltz is as typically Viennese a product as a Wiener Schnitzel, but in point of fact it evolved from the decidedly boisterous "Ländler" of Upper Austria, Bohemia and Bavaria; and it was not until the Congress of Vienna in 1814 that it carried the Austrian capital by storm. And even then the waltz to which the Congress danced was a somewhat stiff and formal affair, a sort of nineteenth-century minuet.

It was Weber who (probably unwittingly) established the classic pattern of the concert waltz (a sequence of five waltzes and a Coda) in his "Invitation to the Waltz" of 1819, but the first waltzes with the characteristic Viennese lilt were the ones with which Schubert regaled his friends at their Schubertiades, and it was these piano waltzes that paved the way for the orchestral, almost symphonic, waltzes of Johann Strauss I and Joseph Lanner. Their characteristic blend of yearning and gay abandon led the nineteen-year-old Wagner, on his first visit to Vienna in 1832, to describe them as "even more potent than alcohol". Two years earlier Chopin had complained that "the Viennese have no time for serious music; Strauss and Lanner are carrying all before them"; an opinion echoed six years later by the extremely serious-minded Robert Schumann, who was surprised and shocked by what he considered the deplorable levity of Viennese music.

Johann Strauss I was born in 1804, three years after his great contemporary and rival Joseph Lanner (1801–1843), with whom he formed a string quintet (himself playing the viola) which performed all over Europe, frequently at village inns, and in Vienna at the Café Rebhuhn, where one of the regulars was Franz Schubert. As time went on the quintet grew into an orchestra, and this was later divided into two small bands, one conducted by Lanner and one by Strauss. Inevitably there was friction, and the two "Waltz Kings" parted company. But sensing that what the public wanted was more and more waltzes, Strauss soon had no fewer than six bands purveying his own compositions. In 1835 he was appointed Director of Music for the Court Balls, but found time to undertake tours of Germany and the Netherlands with a small band, and in 1837 he even had the temerity to challenge the hegemony of Meyerbeer in

Johann Strauss I

Johannes Brahms at about the time he first came to Vienna

Paris, where he was heard and admired by (amongst others) Berlioz. From Paris he went on to London, where he gave a concert at Buckingham Palace (one of no fewer than seventeen in the British Isles), but during a second visit to London in 1838 he was taken seriously ill and returned to Vienna more dead than alive. However, he recovered sufficiently to accept an appointment as bandmaster of a section of the Vienna militia, and it was in this capacity that he composed his masterpiece, the immortal "Radetzky March" that can still be relied upon to bring the house down at any Vienna concert (Field Marshal Radetzky, 1766–1858, was Austria's outstanding military commander during the nineteenth century). In the spring of 1849 Strauss undertook a third visit to London, but in September of the same year he died of scarlet fever in Vienna, aged forty-five.

His son Johann II, born in 1825, though not his father's equal as a player, was far more talented as a composer, and it was his precocity and panache that led to the friction which for some time clouded the relations between father and son. The father was determined that his son should have nothing to do with music, but before he was twenty young Johann was conducting his own band at the Dommayer Casino in Hietzing, thus openly competing against his celebrated father. His first public concert with his own band, which was given in the teeth of his father's opposition, lasted until the small hours and was an uproarious success. In time, father and son came to terms, and when the former died in 1849 his son later was appointed to succeed him as Director of Music for the Court Balls partly on the strength of a successful visit to the St Petersburg Court seven years previously. By the time he was twenty-eight he was maintaining a musical staff of about three hundred, divided up into several orchestras playing simultaneously at a number of different restaurants and ballrooms, he himself rushing from one establishment to the next and sometimes playing and conducting at six or seven different places in one evening. This kind of life obviously called for a manager in the present-day sense, and this he eventually found in the person of Jetty Treffz, whom he married in St Stephen's Cathedral in 1862. Jetty was the perfect helpmate, turning her hand to anything from copying parts to scrutinising contracts or running up "Palatschinken" (pancakes). With Jetty to look after him Johann II was free to concentrate on the waltzes, polkas, galops, etc., that have made his name a household word: "Voices of Spring", "Roses from the South", "Artists' Life". "Wine, Women and Song", "Tales from the Vienna Woods", and the immortal "Blue Danube". At its first performance in 1867 few would have predicted that this masterpiece would one day set the Thames and every other river in the world on fire. Originally it was a choral waltz to words that had nothing whatever to do with the Danube, blue or otherwise: they were a lamentation on the state of the country's finances after the defeat by Prussia in the brief war of 1866! And it was in Paris, not in Vienna, that this superb waltz was first given in a purely orchestral form without the handicap of its vapid text. From Paris it spread the name and fame of Johann Strauss to the four corners of the earth, and nowadays it is not only regarded as the very epitome of what is called Viennese "light" music, whatever that may be, but has even come to be rated by non-Viennese as the equivalent of an Austrian national anthem (the Viennese themselves would probably give their vote to the "Radetzky March").

With the "Blue Danube" Johann Strauss achieved the rare distinction of being a European celebrity who was also admired and respected in his own country and profession. In 1868 the Prince of Wales (later Edward VII) invited him to London, where he gave six concerts at Covent Garden. In Vienna he even won the admiration of the notoriously aloof Johannes Brahms: to the opening bars of one of

Strauss's waltzes inscribed on a lady's fan Brahms added: "Unfortunately not by me, Johannes Brahms." With Richard Wagner relations were even more cordial, possibly because it was Strauss of all people who introduced Vienna to Wagner's music by playing the Prelude to "Tristan und Isolde" at a concert in the Volksgarten. Be that as it may, Wagner publicly expressed his opinion that "Johann Strauss has more music inside that skull of his than anyone else in this century" (except of course Wagner himself).

Although the "Blue Danube" is arguably the most popular waltz ever composed, Strauss had for some time had his eyes on a different horizon, possibly as a result of a meeting with Jacques Offenbach three years earlier. "You ought to try your hand at operetta", Offenbach is said to have advised, "you have all the qualifications for it." The story may or may not be true: for one thing, it is highly unusual, to say the least, for a composer to go out of his way to give gratuitous advice to a potential rival. However, Jetty is known to have turned his head in the same direction, and after one or two false starts Strauss produced his first operetta "Indigo and the forty thieves", now known as "1001 Nights", in 1871. Three years later came his masterpiece "Die Fledermaus", first performed on Easter Sunday 1874 at the Theater an der Wien. It was written in six weeks, and as in the case of many another masterpiece the first performance was a fiasco: it was not until this most Viennese of operettas found its way to Berlin of all places that it scored a sensational success and eventually achieved a run of fifty-eight performances in its first year. Nowadays it is traditionally performed at the Vienna Opera on New Year's Eve.

With the "Blue Danube" and "Die Fledermaus" to his credit Strauss was now more than just a European celebrity: his fame had spread across the Atlantic, and in 1876 he was invited to Boston, where he conducted a massed force of over a thousand performers at a marathon concert in celebration of the centenary of the Declaration of Independence. His own account of the proceedings modestly belittled his personal contribution: "As we all started more or less at the same time, all I had to do was to see that we all finished at the same time." He also visited New York, and took in Italy on his way back to Vienna.

In 1878 his beloved Jetty died at the age of sixty, and in desperation Strauss married a girl thirty-five years younger than himself, with disastrous results. Eventually she left him altogether, and his last wife, who survived him, restored his self-confidence and encouraged him to return to operetta, the results being "A Night in Venice" (1883) and "The Gipsy Baron" (1885), his greatest success since "Die Fledermaus": it ran for eighty-five consecutive performances, an unheard-of achievement in those days. His last, and in many ways his most hilarious operetta "Wiener Blut" is a posthumous concoction assembled by Adolf Müller from miscellaneous fragments of previous works and sketches, and with it the Golden Age of Viennese Operetta came to an end.

In 1888 Strauss returned to his first love and produced what from a purely musical point of view is his finest concert waltz, the "Emperor Waltz". Its introduction has been compared to a splendid staircase leading up to a magnificent ballroom, but underneath the pomp and glitter there are undertones of a sunset glory that foreshadow the music of Gustav Mahler.

Whether Johann Strauss II was fortunate or otherwise in just failing to see the dawn of the twentieth century is a matter of opinion. He died on 3 June 1899 after a life of seventy-four years in the course of which he earned the respect and admiration of both Brahms and Wagner (which was no mean achievement), and of Mahler too. It is fitting that he should be buried near the composer he most aspired to emulate, Franz Schubert; and his statue in the Stadtpark is one of Vienna's most attractive landmarks.

The last word can perhaps be left to the Austrian National Bank, which for many years accorded Johann Strauss the distinction of appearing on its 100 Schilling banknotes, but reserved its 1,000 Schilling notes for Anton Bruckner. So this must be what is meant by "light" music.

As for operetta, the genre evolved from the "musiquettes" of Jacques Offenbach, who made his bow in Vienna in 1858 with a performance (in a German translation) of "Mariage aux lanternes" at a suburban theatre. This was followed two years later by the effervescent "Orpheus in the Underworld", which is still going strong. The first specifically Viennese operetta was "Das Pensionat" by Franz von Suppé (1819–1895) at the Theater an der Wien in 1860. Suppé, who was a relative of Donizetti's, was an exceptionally gifted composer of "light" music, and among his other operettas that are still given from time to time are "Die schöne Galathee" (1865) and "Boccaccio" (1879). Two other lesser contributors to the "Golden Age" were Richard Heuberger (1850–1914), whose "Der Opernball" still features prominently in the repertoire of the Vienna Volksoper; and Carl Millöcker (1842–1899), whose two most successful operettas were "Gräfin Dubarry" (1879) and "Der Bettelstudent" (1882), neither of which is by any means a back number.

If the "Golden Age" of Viennese operetta was dominated by Johann Strauss II, the bright particular star of the "Silver Age" was Franz Lehár (1870–1948). Among other almost equally gifted Silver Age luminaries were Emmerich Kálmán, who was born in 1882, left Vienna in 1938, and died in Paris in 1953, his most successful operettas being "Csardasfürstin" (1915) and "Gräfin Mariza" (1924); Oscar Straus (1870–1954), who achieved immortality in the annals of operetta with the mellifluous "A Waltz Dream" (1907) and "The Last Waltz" (1921); and Leo Fall ("The Dollar Princess", 1907).

Franz Lehár was born at Komorn in Hungary on 30 April 1870. After studying at the Prague Conservatorium he followed in his father's footsteps by going over to military band music, and on one occasion he conducted a concert jointly with Johann Strauss. But his application for a post as a conductor of popular concerts in Vienna was turned down on the grounds that "though Kapellmeister Lehár may be a competent conductor of classical music, he obviously knows nothing about waltzes".

After continuing to serve as a bandmaster in various remote outposts of the Austro-Hungarian Empire, Lehár decided to try his luck in the theatre, and within only ten years of his first essays in the field of operetta he produced his immortal masterpiece "The Merry Widow", first performed at the Theater an der Wien on 30 December 1905. A contemporary critic wrote: "Lehár is obviously of a warm-hearted disposition and music is in his blood. His melodies exude charm and good taste with overtones of a gaiety of a definitely poetic tinge. It is a pleasure to listen to the orchestra under his baton." Where this critic hit the nail on the head is in the matter of orchestration: the orchestral support Lehár gave his melodic line was something quite new in the development of operetta, a blend of the impressionism of Richard Strauss, the timbre of Mahler, and the elegance of Puccini. Even if the "Merry Widow's" immediate successors were not quite up to her standard, Lehár could have lived comfortably on her earnings for the rest of his life. Within five years she was captivating audiences in ten languages and had made over 18,000 appearances, quite overshadowing Lehár's second considerable success "The Count of Luxemburg" (1909).

There is nothing in Lehár of the homely "Ländler" quality of the waltzes of Old Vienna: his "waltz songs" are a further development of the orchestral waltzes of Johann Strauss II. But Lehár was a typical product of the Hungarian element in the multi-racial Dual Monarchy and was inordinately susceptible to Slav and Hungarian, as well as to supra-national, influences. Though he lived in Vienna and thought in Viennese, his music is as multi-racial as was the Empire of which Vienna was the capital.

Paradoxically, it was the disintegration of this Empire in 1918 that led to a kind of Indian summer in Lehár's creative career, culminating in the great triad of "Der Zarewitsch" (1928), "Friederike" (1928), and "The Land of Smiles" (1930). The latter was almost as sensational a success as "The Merry Widow" had been a quarter of a century earlier, and the three are notable as being the first operettas without the conventional happy ending.

Lehár's hopes of emulating Johann Strauss by making an honest woman of operetta, so to speak, by getting her admitted to the stage of the Vienna Opera were at last fulfilled in 1934, when "Giuditta" scored an appreciable success with a cast that included the unforgettable Richard Tauber. But what with the world-wide catastrophe of the Second World War and a progressive deterioration in his health, Lehár wrote nothing after 1939. In 1945 he settled in Zürich, but returned to Austria in 1948 and acquired a villa at Bad Ischl in the Salzkammergut just before his death in October of the same year. The villa is now a museum, and Lehár is also commemorated by an annual summer festival at which his operettas are performed. His Vienna residence at Hackhofer Straße 18 in the Nineteenth District still attracts pilgrims from all over the world, especially as Emanuel Schikaneder, the librettist of "The Magic Flute", once lived in the very same house.

Some words of Lehár's own could serve not only as a fitting epitaph but also as a formulation of what operetta itself is about: "If I have written music that has found an echo among the peoples of the world, it was not merely with the aim of providing entertainment. I wanted to appeal to people's emotions and touch their hearts.".

CHAPTER SEVEN

Johannes Brahms
1833–1897

Like Beethoven, Brahms is qualified by residence and official recognition to be included in the ranks of Viennese composers; but whereas Beethoven settled in Vienna when he was barely out of his teens, and his music is stamped with the unmistakable hallmark of Vienna, the reader would be almost halfway through a biography of Brahms before coming to the North German composer's decision at the age of twenty-nine to make Vienna his permanent home, and one listens in vain for anything specifically Viennese in Brahms's music. Both composers spent exactly the same number of years, thirty-five to be exact, in the Austrian capital, and both brought with them excellent "references". Indeed, it was on personal recommendation rather than by virtue of any outstanding achievement that Vienna made Brahms welcome in 1862, for the only major works he had in his luggage were the two Serenades and the First Piano Concerto which he had performed himself at Hanover in 1859 with Joachim conducting, and again at the Leipzig Gewandhaus five days later, a performance that Brahms described as a "brilliant and resounding failure". But he was able to produce a glowing testimonial from Robert Schumann, whose name carried considerable weight in the musical world, and another decisive factor in Brahms's decision to try his luck in Vienna was the recommendation of the great violinist and conductor Joseph Joachim, who was a native of Kittsee in what is now the Austrian province of Burgenland.

Johannes Brahms was born in Hamburg in 1833 and like Beethoven made an early reputation as a pianist, but it was not until he was eighteen that he took his first faltering steps as a composer. At the age of twenty he embarked upon a venture that was to bear important fruit in his career as a composer: he undertook a tour of Hungary with an expatriate Hungarian violinist named Reményi, a practitioner of the "gipsy fiddler" variety. It was in Hungary that Brahms first met Joseph Joachim, who gave him an introduction to Franz Liszt at Weimar, who in turn recommended him to approach Robert Schumann in Leipzig. Liszt was a good deal more impressed by Brahms than Brahms was by Liszt, and as time went on Brahms developed an implacable hostility to Liszt and to everything he stood for in music. This quarrel with Liszt, which was unfortunately only one of many in which Brahms indulged in his time, was particularly unedifying in that Liszt invariably treated Brahms with his habitual courtesy and charm and did all he could to help the young North German on his way. Brahms also fell out eventually with Reményi, which meant that he had to fall back on the Schumanns, who were by this time in Düsseldorf. Unfortunately Robert Schumann soon died in an asylum, but with his widow Clara Brahms contracted a lifelong friendship, though even with her there were frequent tiffs, due largely to the fact that Clara was fourteen years older than he was and was totally devoid of a sense of humour. Her numerous progeny may well have been a deterrent to any ideas of matrimony Brahms may have been harbouring, though it has frequently been conjectured that his relationship with Clara was the closest he ever sailed to the winds of wedlock, apart perhaps from an earlier episode with a young lady from Göttingen from whom he disentangled himself without the slightest regard for her feelings. It can be assumed that they both had lucky escapes.

Brahms's life in Vienna was outwardly uneventful. Unlike Beethoven, he could nearly always be found at the same address, Karlsgasse 4 near the Karlskirche (the house is no longer standing). An early experience after settling in Vienna was an encounter with Richard Wagner at the latter's villa at Hadikgasse 72 in the Fourteenth District (not far from the Kennedy Bridge), where he was roped in to help copy the parts of "Die Meistersinger" and complied without a murmur. There was a further confrontation at a good-humoured party at the same villa on 6 February 1864. Brahms played some of his piano works and Wagner duly delivered his opinion: "It shows what can be done with the traditional forms by one who knows how to handle them", a verdict that does credit to Wagner's objective judgment. After these initial encounters, relations between Brahms and Wagner steadily deteriorated, and with two such wildly incompatible characters it is difficult to say where the blame lay. After his marriage to Cosima von Bülow, Wagner's aversion to Brahms stiffened, but Brahms sincerely admired Wagner's music though he detested him as a man. In time the two great composers were manoeuvred by their supporters into heading two bitterly opposing factions, the "Bayreuther Blätter" for instance referring to Brahms as "the eunuch of music". And when Wagner died in 1883 Brahms sent a wreath which Cosima did not even bother to acknowledge, on the grounds that "he is not one of us".

Brahms's first concerts in Vienna, both as a pianist and as a composer, were eminently successful, and for once in a way he also succeeded in making a friend, and a very influential one at that, the foremost critic of his time Eduard Hanslick. Within a year Brahms was appointed conductor of the "Singakademie" choir, but resigned after a year to return to Hamburg to be at his mother's deathbed. Music benefited from his experience in the form of the

"Requiem" which he completed three years later. When the first three sections were performed the following year at Vienna's new Musikverein Brahms was deeply wounded by their cool reception, but when the work was first performed in full in Leipzig two years later it scored a notable success. A much more popular work of this same year 1869 was the first set of "Hungarian Dances" originally published as piano duets, like Antonin Dvořák's "Slavonic Dances". A second set followed eleven years later. As their title indicates, they are the fruits of his youthful tour of Hungary with Reményi, but there is nothing about them of the genuine Hungarian idiom later propagated by Béla Bartók and Zoltán Kodály.

Back in Vienna Brahms was still acknowledged and accepted despite his boorish behaviour and deliberate rudenesses. By 1872 he was even appointed to an official position, Artistic Director of the Gesellschaft der Musikfreunde, and following his resignation four years later in order to be absolutely free to compose at leisure he was elected a life member of the committee and invariably sat in the Director's upper box on the left-hand side of the Main Hall of the Musikverein.

A pupil gave the following description of him at this time (i.e. before he grew that great beard): "He was below middle height, and stocky but not corpulent. His fair hair was brushed straight back: he had a high, intellectual forehead, bright blue eyes, a protruding lower lip à la Beethoven, and small hands and feet. He usually wore a short, loose alpaca coat, and a double eyeglass on a thin cord round his neck. He was a great walker and an early riser, about four a.m. in summer."

As a composer, but not as a pianist, Brahms was a late developer, and he was over forty before he could bring himself to complete his first symphony in 1876, after turning it over in his mind for no fewer than fourteen years.

Even as late as 1871 he told the German conductor Hermann Levi, who later conducted the first performance of "Parsifal", that he would never compose a symphony. The first performance of the First Symphony at Karlsruhe in the same year was a qualified success, and once he had taken the plunge Brahms followed it within a year by the Second Symphony, written partly at Pörtschach in Carinthia. It was first performed by the Vienna Philharmonic conducted by Hans Richter in 1877, and its redolence of a Carinthian summer earned it a more immediate success than the rugged First.

Now that Brahms had got his first two symphonies off his chest, Joachim suggested a tour of England, but Brahms could not be bothered to uproot himself from Vienna: instead, he authorised Joachim to perform the First Symphony in acknowledgement of Brahms having been named an honorary Doctor of Music of Cambridge Universitiy.

Another of his finest works inspired by the Pörtschach countryside was the Violin Concerto of 1878, written for Joachim and first performed in Leipzig the same year. This was followed by the "Academic Festival Overture" and its "twin" the "Tragic Overture", written not at Pörtschach but at Bad Ischl in Upper Austria. The former, based on German student-songs, was written for Breslau University in return for the award of an honorary degree of Doc. Phil., while the latter's autumnal mellowness makes it one of the most satisfying of his major orchestral works.

Twenty-one years after his First Piano Concerto, Brahms produced the monumental Second in B Flat. It was first sketched three years previously (1878) after a visit to Italy, though in all conscience there is nothing Italian about this redoubtable work; and it was at Pressbaum, just outside Vienna, that he put the finishing touches to it. He is said to have made it dauntingly difficult in order to deter all but the most proficient pianists from tackling it: at all events he himself was the soloist at the first performance in Budapest in the same year 1881. This work is the first example of a four-movement piano concerto, the second movement having been added because Brahms thought the first movement too simple!

The Second Piano Concerto is in many ways a symphony with piano, and it was to the symphony that Brahms returned in 1883. The Third, arguably the most immediately attractive of the four symphonies, was first performed by the Vienna Philharmonic, the conductor once again being Hans Richter. It was followed the very next year by the massive Fourth Symphony, completed at the Styrian town of Mürzzuschlag, on which Brahms commented to the conductor Hans von Bülow that "the cherries are not sweet here", a hint that the symphony too would be anything but sweet. This time the first performance was not in Vienna but at Meiningen, Germany, Brahms himself conducting.

In 1887, when he was fifty-four, Brahms had an unexpected encounter with Tchaikovsky in Leipzig, after which Tchaikovsky claimed that he had really tried very hard and had been extremely patient with people who told him how much he would enjoy Brahms's music in time. But the time never came: Tchaikovsky admired Brahms's attitude to music, but not the results of it.

In the following year Brahms produced what was to be his last big orchestral work, the Double Concerto for Violin and Cello to commemorate his reconciliation with Joachim, who was only one of the leading musicians of the day with whom Brahms fell out. The list makes formidable reading. His relations with Wagner had gone from bad to worse ever since the two first meetings at the Hadikgasse villa when Brahms was only twenty-nine. In the case of Hugo Wolf the aversion was not entirely mutual: Wolf abhorred Brahms and his music, whereas Brahms merely ignored Wolf's existence. With Liszt, the roles were reversed. Brahms detested Liszt, while Liszt treated Brahms with courtesy and elegance. But the bitterest feud in which Brahms was involved was with Anton Bruckner, who as a resident in Vienna committed the unforgivable offence of constituting a potential rival. The feud was certainly not Bruckner's fault, for Bruckner was essentially a man of peace; but on the death of Wagner in 1883 the "anti-Brahmins" cast around for a new champion to lead them into battle, and their choice fell on poor Bruckner, who was thereby manoeuvred much against his will into an entirely false position. Brahms seemed to go out of his way to be deliberately offensive to Bruckner, referring to Bruckner's sincere religious convictions as "priest-ridden bigotry" and to his symphonies as "symphonic boa-constrictors, the amateurish, confused and illogical abortions of a rustic schoolmaster". On another occasion he derided Bruckner as "a simple soul who will be forgotten a year or two after my death: he owes his fame entirely to me". He even declined to attend Bruckner's funeral at the Karlskirche, but stumped up and down outside the church muttering "It will be my turn soon enough" and already exhibiting unmistakable symptoms of the disease that was to kill him within a year.

It has been said that Brahms, like Clara Schumann, had no sense of humour, but stories still going the rounds in Vienna suggest that he did possess a brand of dry humour that was peculiarly his own. On one occasion for instance an aspiring young soprano on the threshold of her first recital sang some of her programme to Brahms at his home, and then went prattling on about how excited she was: "I've just bought a new dress and new shoes to match." "What a pity I wasn't in time to stop you," was Brahms's encouraging rejoinder. On another occasion, after finishing lunch at his favourite Gasthaus he excused himself to the proprietor: "If there's still anyone on your staff I haven't yet been rude to, please forgive the omission."

It is significant that of Brahms's few friends in the musical world not one constituted any sort of threat to his own supremacy in Vienna. Robert Schumann was dead, and his widow Clara was a pianist and not a composer. Edvard Grieg and Antonín Dvořák he could afford to patronise because they were safely tucked away in Norway and Bohemia respectively. Schubert and Johann Strauss II he allowed himself to admire sincerely because the former was safely dead, and Strauss, apart from operating on a level that rarely impinged on his own, was far too popular to risk alienating. Among works Brahms unreservedly acclaimed were Georges Bizet's "Carmen", Part 2 of Berlioz' "Enfance du Christ", and Verdi's "Requiem", all of which he regarded as works of genius.

Brahms's last years were free from social or material worries of any kind, and his assured financial position allowed him to gratify his predilection for the south, particularly Carinthia. He was held in immense public esteem, and was exposed to a great deal of adulation that was not calculated to improve his affability. His last appearance in public, deathly yellow in the face, was in the Directors' box at a Gesellschaft der Musikfreunde concert at which his Fourth Symphony was played, and he received a tremendous ovation. He died on 3 April 1897 of cancer of the liver, aggravated by a chill caught after arriving too late for Clara Schumann's funeral in Frankfurt the year before: as G. K. Chesterton was always doing, he took the wrong train. His own funeral was almost as elaborate as Beethoven's, and he is appropriately buried near Beethoven and Schubert in the Vienna Central Cemetery. One of the pallbearers at the funeral was Antonín Dvořák.

Johann Strauss II and Johannes Brahms at Bad Ischl

Hugo Wolf

The success of Brahms's works in his lifetime, and the royalties he earned in Vienna, enabled him to lead a leisured and orderly existence. Like Gustav Mahler, he was primarily a "summer composer", preferably in Carinthia or at Bad Ischl. The autumns and winters were reserved for extensive polishing and revising, one of his greatest virtues as a composer being his severe self-criticism, coupled with a natural diffidence that precluded him from venturing on to ground where he was not quite certain of himself, or from trying conclusions with opera. The essential seriousness of this music is a reflection of his fundamentally serious attitude to life in general and to music in particular. It is perhaps his restraint and moderation that make him so popular nowadays in England and Central Europe, whereas in the Latin countries his music is less warmly appreciated.

Technically, Brahms's outstanding quality as a composer was his complete mastery of classical sonata form. He was also unsurpassed as an inventor of variations, notably the orchestral "Variations on a theme by Haydn" and the masterly piano variations on themes by Handel and Paganini. On the other hand, some critics have found him lacking in the spontaneous invention of the earlier Viennese composers. His present popularity in Vienna is due largely to his music being exactly suited to Viennese tastes, not too hot and not too cold; it eschews excitement and seldom commits the unforgivable sin of being boring. It should also be borne in mind that until quite recently there were plenty of people still living in Vienna who could remember Brahms well. The late Bernhard Paumgartner, for instance, President of the Salzburg Festival, used to recall how as a boy he once fell and cut his knee in the Ressel Park (just off the Wiedner Hauptstrasse, not far from where the monument to Brahms now stands), and how he was helped to his feet and dusted down by an elderly looking gentleman with a luxuriant beard.

The view has also been expressed that the history of music would have been much the same if Brahms had never lived. Possibly, but not our enjoyment of it.

CHAPTER EIGHT

Anton Bruckner
1824–1896

When Schubert visited the great monastery of St Florian with Michael Vogl in the summer of 1825 he could not of course know that at the nearby village of Ansfelden another schoolmaster's son like himself was on the eve of celebrating his first birthday and would one day restore the continuity of the Austrian tradition that was to be temporarily interrupted by Schubert's own death.

Anton Bruckner has been the victim of almost as much gross misrepresentation as Schubert. In the first place, he has for some strange reason been coupled with Gustav Mahler, whereas all these two composers have in common is that until comparatively recent times they were virtually unknown outside Central Europe and Holland. The neglect of Bruckner's symphonies in Britain and the United States during the first half of the present century is hard to excuse but easier to explain. Before the Second World War, Anglo-Saxon taste was regaled with the "instant" music of, say, Sibelius, and there would have been some impatience with the leisurely progress of a Bruckner symphony. In an age of speed and quick results the measured dignity and ample proportions of Bruckner's music would have seemed out of place, if not downright boring. Another factor which until recently contributed to Bruckner's eclipse in the Anglo-Saxon world was ignorance. His music is so completely and characteristically Austrian that it cannot be fully savoured without some knowledge of the surroundings and circumstances in which it was written.

Anton Bruckner's place among the immortals is secured by his nine gigantic symphonies, a splendid Te Deum, two full-scale Masses, and curiously enough a solitary String Quintet, plus a considerable quantity of miscellaneous church-music (anthems, motets, etc.). He grew up amid the rolling hills and green forests of the Danube valley near Linz, and like Schubert not only started life as a choirboy but followed in his father's footsteps as a school-teacher at various village schools in Upper Austria. At the age of twenty-four he was appointed organist and choir-master at the Augustinian monastery of St Florian. Deeply religious by nature, he aspired to nothing more rewarding than to be left in peace to work in this secluded environ-ment, but as time went on the necessity of earning a living forced him to move to Linz, where he was appointed Cathedral organist at the age of thirty-two. Five years la-ter he travelled to Vienna to sit for the final examination for an appointment as teacher of harmony and counter-point at the Conservatorium of the Gesellschaft der Mu-sikfreunde, a post which he was to retain until his retire-ment five years before his death. But it was not until seven years after passing the examination that in 1868 he finally plucked up the courage to uproot himself from his beloved Upper Austria and embark upon a new life in Vienna which he was to find far less congenial. By the time he nerved himself to this important decision Bruckner was al-ready forty-four, and apart from a Mass in D minor which had been given in the Hofburg Chapel the year before, Vienna knew precious little about this retiring, profoundly religious Upper Austrian organist. What first struck his new colleagues were his incredible naivety and his insati-able appetite for submitting himself to examinations and amassing sheaves of certificates and diplomas. They knew nothing of the two symphonies he had already composed, Nos o and 1, or of his St Florian Requiem (1849) and

Mass in E minor. His own attachment to the Requiem, which he regarded as "not a bad effort", is attested by the fact that he was revising it as late as 1892, when nearly seventy. The E minor Mass (1866), which was first performed in the New Cathedral in Linz in 1869 (i.e. after the move to Vienna) is a deeply felt and well-written work but is handicapped by the limitations Bruckner imposed upon himself by restricting the accompaniment to wind instruments and dispensing with the organ altogether, because the first performance was to be in front of the Cathedral (i.e. in the open air).

Just before the move to Vienna Bruckner underwent a severe spiritual crisis, and it was in gratitude for being brought safely through it that he wrote the splendid Mass in F minor which was first performed in the Augustinian Church in Vienna in June 1872, Bruckner himself conducting. This was his first important public appearance in Vienna, though the year before he had travelled to London to give organ recitals at the Albert Hall and Crystal Palace, both of which created a profound impression in musical circles. Musically, the F minor Mass is a direct descendant of Schubert's last Mass in E flat.

The two symphonies Bruckner wrote before the move to Vienna contain many of the characteristic features of his mature works. No 0 in D minor owes its unique title to the fact that though Bruckner disowned it at the time it was written (Linz, 1863), he could never bring himself to discard it, and he subjected it to a thorough revision as soon as he settled in Vienna.

Meanwhile, Bruckner had undergone an experience that was to dominate his musical thought for the rest of his days: in 1863 he heard "Tannhäuser" performed in Linz. He also paid a visit to Munich, where he heard "Tristan" and met Richard Wagner personally. The immediate result of Bruckner's introduction to the music of Wagner was his

First Symphony, which was written in 1865–66, but not performed until 1868, when Bruckner himself conducted it in Linz Redoutensaal. After the performance, hopes were expressed by the Upper Austrian authorities that "Bruckner will soon find in the Imperial capital a post worthy of his talent and attainments so as to be able to apply himself at his leisure to his creative aspirations". The post was forthcoming, but not the "leisure". Subsequently, Bruckner subjected this First Symphony to the same treatment as his other symphonies were to undergo: though composed as early as 1865–66 it was thoroughly overhauled in 1877 and again in 1899.

In tracing the stages of Bruckner's development as a symphonic composer it should be borne in mind that he rarely worked continuously on any one work: throughout his career he was constantly interrupting work on a new symphony to go over an earlier one and make far-reaching alterations. It is this practice of his that has caused so much confusion, and even bitter personal feuds, among musicologists over which version of any given symphony is the authentic one. To make matters worse, Bruckner more than once acquiesced in drastic "improvements" executed by conductors who thought they knew more about form and orchestration than Bruckner did; whereas in point of fact it is the symmetry of the architectural structure that is the hallmark of a Bruckner Symphony, notably the Finale of the Fifth Symphony. A Bruckner symphony can be likened to a succession of huge blocks of sound, each developed to a culmination. The noblest movement is usually the Adagio, while the Scherzo invariably brings an unmistakable breath of good Upper Austrian fresh air into the concert-hall. The length of a mature Bruckner symphony varies from sixty to eighty minutes, which is twenty minutes longer than the "heavenly length" of Schubert's last symphony. This unusual length, which is due to a slow pulse that beats once every four bars instead of every single bar, is by no means out of proportion to Bruckner's conception of a symphony: the form is perfectly symmetrical, and to make cuts ruins the entire architectural structure.

Equally characteristic features of a Bruckner symphony are the sudden pauses, as if he had run out of ideas and had no alternative but to stop and start all over again. But here again Bruckner knew perfectly well what he was doing: he envisaged hearing his music performed in great baroque buildings like St Florian, and the pauses are simply to allow the music to roll round their domes and arches, which is why the full effect is largely lost in the concert-hall.

One of Bruckner's students at the Vienna Conservatorium was Gustav Mahler. Bruckner arrived there as a teacher in 1868, Mahler as a student in 1875. Mahler was never one of Bruckner's pupils in the full sense, but despite the difference in their ages and their widely different attitudes to music, Mahler harboured a sincere respect for Bruckner, and in time a genuine friendship developed, especially after Bruckner was appointed a lecturer at Vienna University in 1875. It was in many ways a curious friendship, the only sentiments the two had in common being a whole-hearted admiration of Wagner and an aversion to Brahms. Although Bruckner's lectures were naïve and amiable to the verge of incoherence Mahler dutifully attended them, though somewhat irregularly, in order to spare the older man embarrassment: he cannot possibly have learned very much from them. Sometimes the two would lunch together, Bruckner paying for the beer and Mahler for the rolls; but as Mahler often had no money, there were times when the lunches were limited to beer. A decade or so later, when Mahler was in a position to further Bruckner's cause as a composer, he did so unstintingly: in 1892 for instance he introduced Hamburg to the Te Deum and the Third Symphony, and when the year after Bruckner died Mahler became Director of the Vienna Opera and a conductor of the Philharmonic concerts he seized the opportunity to perform Bruckner's Sixth Symphony in 1899, albeit with unforgivable, and for Mahler quite inexplicable, cuts. In 1901 Mahler conducted Bruckner's Fourth and Fifth Symphonies in Vienna, and in New York in 1908 he initiated a Bruckner series: all nine symphonies were given, and all flopped.

Another stalwart champion of Bruckner's symphonies was Hugo Wolf, who declared in the Journal "Salonblatt" that even one of Bruckner's minor works was "a Chimborazo compared to Brahm's symphonic molehills".

Bruckner's attitude to Brahms has already been outlined: it only remains to add that Bruckner was far too ingenuous to harbour malice against anyone, and the rift was temporarily patched up by members of both camps arranging a meeting between the two protagonists at a Vienna Gasthaus, where they both ordered the same dish—smoked gammon and dumplings—the only discordant note being Bruckner's habit of addressing Brahms as "Doctor", which annoyed Brahms intensely. Thereafter, Brahms reverted to his saturnine hostility, and Bruckner kept himself to himself.

Bruckner's Second Symphony (1872) is a somewhat disappointing work in that it shows little or no advance on Nos 0 and 1, though at its first performance by the Vienna Philharmonic in 1873 it scored a qualified success. Bruckner had great hopes of the revised version of 1877, but it still remains the least often performed of his symphonies, except No 0.

Paradoxically, the splendid Third Symphony dedicated to Wagner was a complete fiasco at its first performance at a Philharmonic concert on Boxing Day 1877, and only about a dozen stalwart supporters sat it through to the end, among them the seventeen year old Mahler, who hastened to console Bruckner and later arranged a piano score of it. Of all Bruckner's symphonies, none has suffered more grievously from totally unwarranted tampering by well-meaning "friends and counsellors", with the result that three different versions have been in circulation at one time or another. Nowadays, the usual practice is to play the original version of Bruckner's symphonies, apart perhaps from minor modifications sanctioned by the composer himself. Unfortunately, the amiable and conciliatory Bruckner allowed himself to be talked into all sorts of cuts and alterations of which in his heart of hearts he cannot have approved. In the case of the Third Symphony however the first performance of the third version in 1890 by the Vienna Philharmonic under Hans Richter was a triumphant success. "I was recalled at least twelve times", Bruckner wrote. The humiliation of 1877 was at long last wiped out.

The Fourth Symphony in E flat, the "Romantic", is perhaps the most universally popular of Bruckner's symphonies, especially the "hunting" Scherzo. It was completed in 1880, when Bruckner was fifty-eight, and once again the first performance was by the Vienna Philharmonic conducted by Richter. Later, it was subjected to the inevitable revisions, and Bruckner was still "having another look at it" as late as 1890. One of the revised versions has found its way to the Music Department of the Columbia Universities Library in New York. The Fourth was the first of Bruckner's symphonies to have been favourably received from the very first: it is "easy on the ear" and poses no metaphysical problems.

The superb Fifth Symphony is the most architectural of Bruckner's symphonies and from a purely musical point of view the richest, which makes it all the more poignant that, along with the Sixth and the unfinished Ninth, Bruckner never heard it. The first draft was completed in 1876, before Bruckner went off to Bayreuth to hear the "Ring", at a time when his spirits were at their lowest. In a letter to a friend the year before he had written: "I suppose I shall just keep on piling up debts until I end up by enjoying the fruits of my labours in prison, ruminating on the lunacy of ever having allowed myself to be persuaded to move to Vienna in the first place. It has cost me a thousand florins a year, and in return I get absolutely nothing, not even a Government grant. I can't even afford to have my Fourth Symphony copied." And a month later: "All the joy and pleasure have gone out of my life, it seems utterly pointless and futile." As so often, from this access of abject despair there emerged a monumental masterpiece, and a masterpiece with a glorious Finale, usually the movement that cost Bruckner most trouble. The customary revision was embarked upon in 1877 and completed within a year. For some reason Bruckner then put the symphony aside, and it languished among his piles of papers until two years before his death, when its first performance under Franz Schalk in Graz made a tremendous impact. By then however Bruckner was too frail to make the journey to Graz, and his last reserves of strength were being expended on trying to complete the Ninth Symphony. Like so many of his other symphonies, the Fifth has been subjected to numerous amendments and above all cuts, one conductor (who shall be nameless) perpetrating the atrocity of cutting no fewer than 122 bars out of the Finale! With no other symphony of Bruckner's is it so important to perform his original version, and no other symphony manifests so unequivocally his complete mastery of form, structure and orchestration, especially in the tremendous Chorale in the Finale.

The contrast between the mighty Fifth and Bruckner's next work could hardly be more unexpected. His only published contribution to chamber-music, the String Quintet completed in July 1879, is seldom performed, largely because of the exacting technical demands it makes on the performers. As well as being extremely difficult to play, it is also elusive to listen to, and intense concentration is called for. As with most of the symphonies, the finest movement is the Adagio, which a contemporary critic ranked with the slow movements of Beethoven's last quartets.

The Sixth Symphony, completed in 1881 after two years' work, is one of the less popular of the nine (or ten), but it has the usual lovely Adagio. It is a straightforward and uncomplicated work that has suffered from being overshadowed by its two "big brothers", the Fifth and the Seventh.

The Seventh Symphony in E major is the most frequently played of all Bruckner's symphonies, and like the Fourth constitutes an admirable introduction to his idiom. For one thing, it has been less interfered with than any of the others, and for another it has an Adagio which is generally held to be the finest single movement Bruckner ever wrote. He had been to the Bayreuth Festival of 1882, so that the news of Wagner's death came as a tremendous shock to him, a shock which is reflected in the last two and a half pages of the obituary Coda of the Adagio. Bruckner's veneration of Wagner was unbounded, and it was to raise funds for a Wagner memorial that Arthur Nikisch conducted the first performance of the Seventh in Leipzig (Wagner's birthplace) in 1884, one year after Wagner's death. Its immediate success established Bruckner as a celebrity far beyond the boundaries of Austria-Hungary, though he himself was the last to realise it. One critic went so far as to accuse Austria of having deliberately kept to herself one of the world's greatest symphonic masters.

The close thematic affinity between the fourth bar of the Adagio of the Seventh Symphony and the closing section of the Te Deum of 1884, is due to the fact that Bruckner interrupted work on the Te Deum to write the Symphony, a further example of his curious reluctance to concentrate on one work at a time. The first public performance of the Te Deum was at a Gesellschaft der Musikfreunde concert conducted by Hans Richter, and its success was so immediate that even in Bruckner's lifetime it was given in such widely separated cities as Christiania (now Oslo) and Cincinnatti. It is indeed a splendid and deeply felt work: Bruckner himself referred to it as "the pride of my life".

The colossal Eighth Symphony, finished in September 1887 when Bruckner was sixty-three, represents the glorification of temporal "might, majesty, dominion and power" and is appropriately dedicated to the Emperor Franz Joseph, who duly defrayed the costs of publication. Owing to its inordinate length, between eighty and eighty-five minutes according to who is conducting, it usually has the programme all to itself. It must be the only example in musical history of a symphony being revised before ever being performed. As soon as he had finished the orginal version he sent it to Hermann Levi, the conductor earmarked for the first performance. Though enthusiastic about the Seventh, Levi could not make head or tail of the Eighth, and his adverse verdict, corroborated as it was by other friends of Bruckner's, reduced the composer to the verge of prostration. However, he stoically set about a complete revision, and the first performance in December 1892, with Hans Richter once again conducting the Vienna Philharmonic, was a tremendous triumph. Hugo Wolf, always one of Bruckner's staunchest supporters, wrote to a friend:

"This symphony is the work of a Titan, and in grandeur, breadth of vision and fertility of invention surpasses even his previous symphonies. Notwithstanding the usual Cassandra-like prophecies of woe, even from those in the know, its success was almost without precedent . . . and the storm of applause at the end was like some elemental manifestation of Nature." But the vitriolic and uninhibited critic Eduard Hanslick, the champion of the "Brahmins" and an implacable opponent of Wagner and Bruckner, was less enthusiastic: "If this nightmare caterwauling is the music of the future, which I find hard to believe, then I do not envy the future." It only remains to add that Hanslick was the prototype of Wagner's Beckmesser in "Die Meistersinger"; Wagner originally called him "Hans Lick".

Though Bruckner started work on his Ninth Symphony in 1887 it was still without a Finale when he died nine years later. If the Eighth is the glorification of earthly power, the Ninth is a symphonic apotheosis and is dedicated to Almighty God. It was written on the eve of a new century, during a decade which was as clearly defined a musical watershed as Haydn's last years, the period between Mozart and Beethoven. In a world very different from Bruckner's, Richard Strauss was striking a new note with his symphonic poems, Debussy was well-established, Mahler was exploring the uttermost limits of tonality, and Mascagni and Leoncavallo were paving the way for Puccini. As the work slowly took shape Bruckner became obsessed with the vital necessity of finishing it, but it was not to be. He had lived for nineteen years at Hessgasse 7 near Schottenring, but as his health steadily deteriorated he was granted a "grace and favour" residence in the grounds of the Upper Belvedere, where it was hoped the cleaner air would do him good. When at last he was forced to realise he would never find the strength to embark upon the Finale, let alone complete it, Bruckner sanctioned the use of the "Te Deum" as a Finale, but nowadays the work is usually given as a three-movement symphony on its own, the second movement being a Scherzo like Olympian laughter, and the third a profoundly moving Adagio.

In the last decade of his life Bruckner was accorded in Vienna the respect and admiration he had always enjoyed in Upper Austria; but after his death in Vienna at the age of seventy-two his body was returned to the monastery of St Florian from where he had first set out on his career: and there it now rests under the nave directly below the organ-loft in the great church.

CHAPTER NINE

Hugo Wolf
1860–1903

Of all the great Viennese composers, Hugo Wolf must be the least familiar to the average concert-goer, the reason being that not only is his output virtually confined to Lieder, but these Lieder can only be fully appreciated by a complete understanding of the German text. Wolf's importance in the history of music lies in his having created a completely new form of Lied, a kind of dramatic, symphonic miniature in which the poem and its musical setting are indivisible, in accordance with Wagner's precept that a song "should be as inseparable from the words as from the music."

Hugo Wolf was born in 1860 at Windischgratz (today Slovenj Gradec in Slovenia) in what was then an exceedingly remote corner of Styria. His father, like his fathers before him, was a leather craftsman, and the family were reasonably well off. Every evening after work there was music in the home, so it was in a definitely musical atmosphere that Hugo spent his formative years; and it was by his father that he was given his first piano and violin tuition. Unfortunately however his conscientious parent showed a surprising lack of understanding in sending the boy to an ordinary grammar school, which Hugo attended with extreme reluctance. In fact he was by no means lazy or stupid, but from 1870 till 1875 all attempts to get him to concentrate on his studies at schools in Graz and Maribor and at St. Paul's Abbey in Carinthia proved abortive. Already one of his salient characteristics, a resolute determination to go his own way, was beginning to assert itself, but in a letter to his father written about this time he struck a conciliatory note: "I was sorry to read in your last letter that you still can't agree to my taking up music. Very well, then: I'll give up music entirely and apply myself to a profession... But I am so passionately in love with music, it is food and drink to me. However, since you are definitely against my becoming a serious musician (not a musical hack as you seem to imagine), I will conform. I only pray to God that your eyes will not be opened later on when it is too late for me to go back to music. From your last letter I could see quite clearly that in your eyes a professional musician's is a pretty low form of life. You pity me for wanting to become one: I pity you for not letting me."

But in 1875, when he was fifteen, the boy's fondest hopes were realised; an aunt of his volunteered to put him up in Vienna, and full of eager expectations he presented himself at the Conservatorium, but soon found to his dismay that he was way ahead of the plodding, routine tuition of his teachers in piano and harmony. Once again he found himself in the grip of his old enemy, frustration, until an obscure prank perpetrated in his name by some fellow students led to his expulsion from the Conservatorium in 1877. The only benefit he derived from his two years there was the friendship of one of his contemporaries, Gustav Mahler.

Between September 1875 and May 1879 he emulated Beethoven by lodging at no fewer than twenty-one different addresses in Vienna, until a bright new star appeared in his firmament, Richard Wagner. "His wonderful music has completely bowled me over," he confessed in a letter, "I am now a confirmed Wagnerite." Hour after hour Wolf would stand waiting outside the Hotel Imperial where Wagner was staying, indifferent to the icy cold as long as

Anton Bruckner

Gustav Mahler

there was a hope of catching a glimpse of his idol, or of opening his carriage door for him, after which he would dash round to the Opera in order to be the first to open the same door when the great man arrived there. For the rest of his life Wolf proudly cherished a few trivial, off-hand words Wagner once addressed to him; and when at the age of twenty-three he heard of Wagner's death he was inconsolable.

Wolf's compositions during this early period were those of a composer still feeling his way, and every effort, his own as well as his friends', to put him in the way of scraping a bare living through some sort of position as a correpetitor or copyist was nullified by his inability to hold down any "steady" job. He did succeed in landing a post as Assistant Kapellmeister at the Landestheater in Salzburg, but was obliged to resign after only two months because instead of training the chorus in their operettas he played them Wagner. In the autumn of 1884 however influential friends were instrumental in procuring him a position as music critic on a not very distinguished publication entitled "Salonblatt", and this post he actually managed to hold down for three years, easily his longest period in continuous employment. But it must be admitted that his criticisms were not always entirely objective, and his attitude to Brahms was particularly unjust. He referred, for instance, to a colleague who supported Brahms against Wagner as a "journalistic gutter-snipe" (Wolf was never one to mince words).

The consequences of this outspokenness were not long in making themselves felt: to whatever quarter he submitted a work it was rejected. In 1884 the Rosé Quartet turned down a string quartet of his, and in 1886 a rehearsal of the tone-poem "Penthesilia", his only orchestral work, broke up amid derisive laughter and the sarcastic comment of the conductor Hans Richter: "I just wanted to set eyes on the fellow who dared to write in such a fashion about Meister Brahms." In those days Brahms was a "sacred cow" in Vienna, and to criticise him was tantamount to blasphemy.

Wolf's career as a critic was terminated by the sudden death of his father in the spring of 1887. The bare chronological record of what now ensued within the space of a few years is almost beyond belief. On 16 February 1888, in the seclusion of Perchtoldsdorf, he composed the first of his "Mörike Lieder". By 18 May forty-three more Lieder had been added; between 31 August and 10 October, that is to say in forty-one days, he completed nine more at Unterach am Attersee as well as setting twelve poems by Eichendorff; and on 27 October he became engrossed in Goethe, completing fifty settings by 12 February 1889, including "Anakreons Grab", "Prometheus", and "Ganymed". In between times, as it were, he wrote in three days (2–4 May 1887) one of his most attractive works, the exquisite "Italienische Serenade" for string quartet, and five years later made an arrangement of it for small orchestra and solo viola.

A second creative explosion followed towards the end of 1889. On 2 October he composed one final setting of Goethe as a sort of afterthought, and a week later started work at Perchtoldsdorf on the "Spanisches Liederbuch", completing the forty-four Lieder by 27 March 1890. Autumn seems to have been Wolf's favourite season for composition, and in the autumn of the same year 1890 came the first seven Lieder of Volume I of the "Italienisches Liederbuch".

The genesis of the "Italienisches Liederbuch" is a typical example of the erratic flow of Wolf's inspiration. After these first seven Lieder in September and October 1890 there ensued a hiatus of over a year, after which the remaining fifteen Lieder of Volume I came pouring out in a matter of twenty-five days in December 1891. Then for the next few years his inspiration dried up completely, and letters written about this time paint an agonising picture of the misery of sterility. At times he was tormented by doubts as to whether he would ever get going again, and it was not until the spring of 1896, i.e. four and a half years after the completion of Volume I, that he was surprised by the preliminary rumblings of a new creative storm. The trickle soon swelled into a torrent, and all the twenty-four Lieder of Volume II were finished off at Perchtoldsdorf in the incredibly short space of thirty-seven days (25 March–30 April 1896). During these creative eruptions two Lieder in one day were nothing unusual, thirty-four times to be precise, 24 February 1888 for instance being the birthday of both "Elfenlied" and "Der Gärtner". During these recurrent bouts of inspiration "his whole being seemed to be on fire, and he was borne on a flood-tide of inspiration clamouring to be released and given form and substance".

For some years a new idea had kept nagging at Wolf —an opera. There had been frantic searches for a libretto (even "The Tempest" was considered), but it was four years before his inspiration was kindled by a text concocted from Alarcón's "El sombrero de tres picos" (The three-cornered hat) by a Viennese writer named Rosa Mayreder. Characteristically, Wolf plunged head first into this new project: starting work at Perchtoldsdorf on 1 April 1895 he finished the full score by 18 December in the complete solitude of a small hunting-lodge at Matzen near Brixlegg in Tyrol. The opera was eventually entitled "Der Corregidor".

It was one thing to compose on opera, but quite another to get it accepted. The Vienna Opera rejected it, so did Berlin and Prague. But Mannheim accepted it, and it was there that on 7 Juni 1896 Wolf heard it for the first and only time. Its success was by no means inconsiderable, and it was given a second time before the end of the season; but by the time it was revived at Strasbourg in 1898 he was too ill to travel, and by 1904, when it at long last reached Vienna, he was dead.

After twenty-one years in Vienna Wolf at last found a home of his own at Schwindgasse 3, not far from the Karlskirche; and in 1897 Gustav Mahler was appointed Director of the Vienna Opera, so in view of their friendship at the Conservatorium Wolf hastened to offer him "Der Corregidor". Mahler promised to put it on, but when the official programme for the coming season eventually appeared, "Der Corregidor" was not on the list. This was the most shattering blow of Wolf's life: he suffered a complete breakdown, and the disease that was ultimately to prove fatal asserted itself almost overnight. While still in a state of euphoria over Mahler's appointment he had composed the first scenes of a second opera called "Manuel Venegas", and it was in a similar transport of fancy that he played them over to some friends of his at Mödling on 19 September 1897. Suddenly he broke off, moved away from the piano, and announced that he had been appointed Director of the Vienna Opera. With some difficulty his friends brought him back to Vienna, and after a day or two he was taken to an asylum, where for a time his hallucinations became even more fantastic. After a while however he seemed to return to normal, and on 24 January 1898 he was discharged as "cured". Ashamed and embarrased, Wolf avoided his former friends and haunts, and embarked upon an introspective journey through northern Italy before accepting an invitation from the Köchert family, the famous Viennese jewellers, to enjoy on Lake Traun in Upper Austria the peace and quiet he so sorely needed. But in October his symptoms reappeared, culminating in an attempt at suicide from which he was saved in the nick of time. At his own request he was then committed to a Vienna asylum where, after languishing for four years and four months in an ever darkening cloud of insanity, he died on 22 February 1903, aged forty-three.

CHAPTER TEN

Gustav Mahler
1860–1911

"Mahler? Heard a piece of his a day or two ago: can't say I liked it much, couldn't get the hang of it at all. A bit too modern for me."

Outside Central Europa, this was the average concert-goer's reaction to Mahler before the Second World War, and performances of Mahler's symphonies were few and far between, despite all the efforts of Bruno Walter and one or two other devoted pioneers; while in Austria the growing appreciation of his true stature was obliterated in 1938 by the Nazi ban on his music. Since 1945 however his popularity has increased by leaps and bounds, and in the eyes, or rather ears, of the younger generation he now ranks as one of the very great symphonic composers. Concert promoters too have found that "there's money in Mahler". These incidentally were developments Mahler himself foresaw: "Meine Zeit wird kommen", he used to say, "My time will come" and how right he was! The older generation however is still not quite sure, and today, over sixty years after his death, Mahler is still not everybody's cup of tea (what composer is for that matter?). There are still plenty of regular concert-goers who find his music at best boring and at worst unintelligible.

As a composer Gustav Mahler was a typical product of the turn of the century, when Vienna was still the capital of a multi-racial Empire, the magnet to which artists of talent or ambition (or both) were irresistibly drawn. He was born outside the boundaries of what is now the Republic of Austria, his birthplace being the small village of Kaliště on the borders of Moravia and Bohemia. Shortly after his birth the family moved to the nearby town of Jihlava on the direct road from Prague to Vienna. Gustav Mahler was one of twelve children, most of whom died in infancy. Young Gustav's musical gifts began to manifest themselves at a very early age, so much so that his father decided to take him in person to Vienna, where he eventually secured the boy's admission to the Conservatorium at the age of fifteen. During his three years there Mahler was on friendly terms with his contemporary Hugo Wolf, and after leaving the Conservatorium with a diploma he put in intermittent appearances at Anton Bruckner's lectures at the University, but if he did venture to try his own hand at composition, the essays have not survived. His first extant composition, "Das klagende Lied", was an elaborate affair which he himself designated as "an opera in three parts": he entered it for the Beethoven Prize of the Gesellschaft der Musikfreunde, but Brahms and the critic Hanslick between them saw to it that it was turned down. Many years later, in 1898 to be precise, Mahler rearranged it for the second time as a Cantata based on Grimm's Fairy Tales, and conducted its first performance at a Philharmonic concert in 1901.

In order to arrive at a proper appreciation of Mahler's contribution and attitude to music, it is essential to have a clear idea of the literary and artistic trends in the new world in which he was about to take his place; a world in which figures such as the writers Hugo von Hofmannsthal, Arthur Schnitzler and Stefan Zweig; and the painters Gustav Klimt, Egon Schiele and the youthful Oskar Kokoschka were already making their mark; a world in which the motor-car and the cinema were beginning to work their social revolution, and traditional values were going down like ninepins.

Although Mahler went back to pre-Wagnerian times in choosing his means of expression, and although he clung to tonality all his life, he was responsible for a great many innovations in symphonic music. The transparency of his instrumentation, which renounces all superfluous accessories and aims only at enhancing the clarity of the musical substance; the concentration with which his ideas are stated; the unyielding persistence of melodic line; all these are also essential features of the "New Viennese School" that was just emerging in the persons of Arnold Schönberg, Anton von Webern, and Alban Berg, all devoted admirers of Mahler's music and fully aware of how much they owed him.

On leaving the Conservatorium Mahler decided to make a career as a Kapellmeister, and after some years of frustration and hardship at Bad Hall, Ljubljana and Olomouc which placed a severe strain on a temperament that was resolutely averse from any form of compromise he secured his first important engagement at the Opera Haus in Kassel (1883–1885). After short spells in Prague and Leipzig he was appointed Director of the new Royal Opera in Budapest, and during his three years there (1888–1891) he made his debut as a composer-conductor, conducting the first performance of his First Symphony in 1889. Two years later however political developments in Hungary made a change of Director inevitable, and after arranging for his contract to be prematurely terminated he went as principal Kapellmeister to Hamburg, where he stayed five years, during which he contracted a firm friendship with a young conductor named Bruno Walter, and completed his Second and Third Symphonies.

1897 was Mahler's year of destiny: two years after being received into the Roman Catholic Church he was appointed Deputy Director of the Vienna Opera, and within a matter of months succeeded Wilhelm Jahn as Director.

And so while still on the right side of forty he had reached the goal on which his eyes had been set from the beginning.

At the Vienna Opera, where Directors had hitherto come and gone with unpredictable rapidity, his ten years at the helm (1897–1907), as well as being a far longer period than most of his predecessors lasted, were a Golden Age. With unflagging energy and an uncompromising idealism in which his colleagues were willy-nilly caught up, he transformed the Vienna Opera from just a place of elegant entertainment into the finest institution of its kind in the world. He himself never for one moment doubted his ability to storm the heights, both as Director and as a composer. His collaboration with the stage-designer Alfred Roller was something unique in the annals of opera and has since become legendary. Roller possessed an uncanny flair for the exact realisation of Mahler's ideas, insisting on an uncluttered stage and introducing a symbolic use of colour in Wagner, notably in an epoch-making production of "Tristan und Isolde" which was as complete a realisation as possible of what Wagner called a "Gesamt-kunstwerk", a synthesis of all the arts. The younger generation were fascinated and their elders were overawed, even to the extent of sitting through uncut Wagner without a murmur. Singers, in most cases for the first time in their lives, awoke to the fact that they were now required to be able to act as well as sing, and subordinates who refused, or were unable, to toe the line were ordered to quit. As an administrator, Mahler showed as little regard for tradition and convention as he did in artistic matters. He was no respecter of persons or reputations, and with his celebrated dictum "Tradition ist Schlamperei" ("tradition is an excuse for slovenliness") he eradicated the complacency and restrictive practices of decades. The house-lights were extinguished while the curtain was up, the claque was suppressed, and once the Overture had started late-comers were not allowed in until the end of Act I. And everyone—officials, audiences and singers—capitulated to his dynamic personality. His only setback was his failure to persuade the Court officials to relax their ban on Richard Strauss's "Salome".

From 1898–1901 Mahler also conducted the traditionally conservative Philharmonic concerts, into which he promptly proceeded to inject a fair modicum of "new" music—Bruckner, Dvořák, Richard Strauss, etc. His dismissal from this post in 1901, after only three years, was the first indication that opposition to his draconian methods was gathering momentum; and from now on he was subjected to a steadily mounting barrage of criticism and intrigue. Not that he minded very much: he was completely sure of himself, as impervious to malice or criticism, even to intrigue, as he was to misunderstanding or even to no understanding at all. But by 1907 he was just sick and tired of constantly beating his head against the wall, even though he may still have felt that he was making a hole in the wall. A contemporary wrote that "only an intellect of infinite innocence, and totally impervious to material considerations, could have succeeded in running Vienna's Imperial Opera for over ten years as if we were back in Athens during the Golden Age of Pericles". So in the end he just gave up: in his heart of hearts he felt there was nothing more he could do; or as he himself put it to Bruno Walter: "During my ten years here I have paced out my full circle:" No doubt he was eventually toppled by the vortex of intrigues concocted by mean-minded mediocrities in high places, but his own tactlessness, refusal to compromise, and lack of social affability also played their part in his downfall. To quote Bruno Walter again: "A life crowded with an infinite variety of human relationsship failed to equip him with even the most elementary social polish." So in 1907 he voluntarily departed from the scene of his greatest triumphs and accepted a wonderfully generous offer from the Metropolitan Opera in New York, where he was even provided with an orchestra of his own which eventually became the New York Philharmonic Symphony Orchestra (half a century later another celebrity of Austrian origin was to make his mark at the "Met", Sir Rudolf Bing). But the idealism and elan of his Vienna days were burned out, and he accepted standards and conditions in America (cuts in Wagner for instance) that he would never for one moment have countenanced at the Vienna Opera. It was as if he no longer cared. He was still conscientious, but no longer compelling.

The summer months, which were almost the only time he could devote to composition, were invariably spent in Austria-Hungary. Until the death of his parents in 1889 he used so spend most of his holidays at Jihlava, but later he preferred Steinbach am Attersee in Upper Austria, where his Second, Third und Fourth Symphonies were written. In 1902 he married the daughter of a well-known landscape painter, the celebrated beauty Alma Schindler who as Alma Mahler-Werfel became a social celebrity in the United States. In the same year he acquired a property at Maiernigg on the Wörthersee in Carinthia. Here he could devote himself solely to composition, and it was here that for the next four years he turned out a symphony every summer (No 5,6,7 and 8).

And so to the fateful year 1907, when Mahler's whole life threatened to crumble. First, there was the death of his elder daughter in July at the age of five, and before the year was out his doctor diagnosed a serious heart complaint that entailed a complete change in Mahler's way of life. The lover of Nature, of long walks and mountain-climbing, was from now on condemned to spare himself every possible exertion, and even if he had not already resigned he would have been unable to continue at the Vienna Opera, where he conducted for the last time in October 1907. During his three and a half years in New York Mahler still returned to Europe every summer, and it was at Toblach in South Tyrol that he composed his Ninth Symphony (1909) and started on a Tenth (1910) as well as completing what may well be his finest work, "Das Lied von der Erde" (1908), a symphony for tenor and alto (or baritone) and orchestra. After travelling to Munich in September 1910 to conduct the first performance of his gigantic Eighth Symphony, an occasion which was the culmination of his career as a composer-conductor, Mahler returned to New York, where he conducted his last concert on 21 February 1911. Following a severe attack of angina pectoris he was persuaded to make the journey to Paris, where it was hoped that his life could be saved by special treatment, but it soon became clear that his ailment was incurable, and at his own earnest request he was brought back to Vienna, where after six days in a sanatorium he died on 18 May 1911, aged fifty-one. He is buried in Grinzing cemetery.

Even in his very earliest works Mahler's highly personal style is unmistakable. It is as if he were speaking the language of tomorrow with the vocabulary of yesterday. The range of his emotional scale is prodigious: at times he seems to be breathing the same air as Schubert, while at others he rivals even the frenetic ferocity of Richard Strauss's "Elektra", but without ever overstepping the bounds of tonality. He once observed that writing a symphony was like creating a whole world with all the technical means at his disposal. But his symphonies are not "programme music" in the sense that Liszt's or Richard Strauss's symphonic poems are: they may reflect, or suggest, metaphysical concepts, moods or fancies, but they do not describe or illustrate actual episodes.

An ardent idealist of Mahler's intensity was bound to be deeply disturbed by his own visions, and the greater part of his life was an unceasing quest for anodynes to assuage the dark fancies that kept crowding in on him, as for instance in the Second Symphony and even more threateningly in the Eighth. It should not be forgotten that Sigmund Freud, whose work on the interpretation of dreams ("Traumdeutung") appeared in 1900, was more than just an acquaintance of Mahler's. The expression in musical terms of the most profound mystical experiences; a heartfelt love of Nature; uncompromising sincerity and deep religious conviction: these were the basic ingredients of Mahler's personality and life's work.

Mahler's nine symphonies fall into two distinct groups: I–IV belong as unmistakably to the nineteenth century as V–IX do to the twentieth. Considering the number of years Mahler spent in Vienna it is astonishing that he never conducted any of his symphonies there, and not one of them was given its first performance in Vienna during his lifetime, for it was not until 1912, a year after his death, that Vienna heard the world premiere of the Ninth Symphony conducted by Bruno Walter. A quarter of a century later, just as conservative Vienna was beginning to come to terms with Mahler's music, the Nazis imposed a total ban on Mahler and everything to do with him: even the Mahler Strasse opposite the Opera House was renamed "Meistersinger Strasse"!

Mahler's first important work after "Das klagende Lied" was the "Lieder eines fahrenden Gesellen" (1883–1885), a cycle of four songs with orchestral accompaniment describing an unhappy love-affair in the folk-song idiom to which he was already attracted. The affinity with Schubert's "Die schöne Müllerin" and "Die Winterreise" cycles is obvious. Two of the songs form some of the thematic material of the First Symphony (1888): the second song,

"Ging heut' morgen übers Feld", a description of a leisurely ramble during the gradual awakening of a spring morning, becomes the main theme of the first movement; while the melancholy close of the fourth song forms the contrasting middle section of the dark and bitter irony of the third movement. The stirring Finale symbolises the triumph of "Paradiso" over "Inferno".

With this first symphony off his chest Mahler reverted to songs with orchestral accompaniment, the "Zwölf Lieder aus 'Des Knaben Wunderhorn'" composed in Hamburg between 1892 and 1895. "Des Knaben Wunderhorn" is a miscellaneous three-volume assortment of old German nursery rhymes and folk-songs, first published in 1806. Three of these songs are included in Mahler's next three symphonies, and it is significant that he returned to this same collection for two of the "Sieben Lieder aus letzter Zeit" (1899–1903).

In the *Second Symphony*, written at Steinbach am Attersee in 1894, the last two of the five movements follow Beethoven's precedent by introducing the human voice, the unpretentious and artless contralto song "Urlicht" from the "Wunderhorn" leading straight into a grandiose vision of the Resurrection, with a final chorus "Auferstehn, ja auferstehn", a free adaptation of verses by Klopstock that expresses most movingly a firm belief in the immortality of the soul: "I shall die in order that I may live." Mahler himself wrote: "For the Finale of my Second Symphony I ploughed through an immense amount of literature, including the Bible . . . I had been toying for a long time with the idea of a choral Finale, but the thought that I might be accused of imitating Beethoven always held me back. Then came Hans von Bülow's death and I went to his funeral in Hamburg, which exactly matched the mood of the symphony I was working on; and as the choir intoned the words "Auferstehn" (rise again) I realised in a flash that my problem was solved and all I had to do was to put my thoughts into music ... It's always the same with me, I can only compose when I am deeply moved, and I am only deeply moved when I am composing."

The keynote of the *Third Symphony*, written at Steinbach in 1896, is the composer's love of Nature, expressed on the same lines as in Beethoven's "Pastorale". For variety of musical content its six movements are the richest of Mahler's symphonies: it is full of surprises at every turn. The first movement is almost as long as the other five put together. The fourth movement is built around a "Wunderhorn" song for alto solo, and the fifth, which includes another "Wunderhorn" song, calls for women's and boys' choirs as well as the alto solo. In view of the widespread popularity of this symphony at the present time, it is hardly credible that after the first Vienna performance in 1904 a "critic" opined that "for perpetrating a thing like this the man ought to spend a year or two behind bars".

The *Fourth Symphony* (1900), also completed at Steinbach, has much in common with the Third, and is probably the most popular and frequently performed of the nine. It is also the shortest (about fifty minutes) and can be recommended as a thoroughly rewarding introduction to Mahler's idiom, being imbued by the same straightforward enjoyment of life as the Third. There are no complications, no stresses; and the orchestration is pruned to almost Mozartian transparency. Once again Mahler turns to the human voice, a soprano this time, in the Finale, which is a child's view of Heaven from the "Wunderhorn" collection, a view not unlike that of the child who thought Heaven would be like eating ice-cream to the sound of a trumpet. Mahler himself considered the Adagio the finest single movement he ever wrote, and few will feel disposed to contradict him.

Although the *Fifth Symphony* was completed at Maiernigg within two years of the Fourth, it represents a very pronounced departure from the style of its predecessors. The Fifth and the two following symphonies dispense with the human voice and form a compact and coherent triad, a subjective appraisal of Mahler's whole attitude to life. The most immediately attractive movement of the Fifth is the all too short Adagietto for harp and strings only: it is sometimes performed on its own, but this is a practice that is a flagrant violation of Mahler's explicit instructions.

The *Sixth Symphony* (Maiernigg 1904) is a complete contrast: it was as if Mahler had already foreseen the calamities that were to strike him down three years later. It is the most difficult and at the same time the most personal of his symphonies in that it makes no concessions and does not attempt to conceal the prevailing mood of introspective pessimism. Of the four movements the Finale is by far the longest (its 882 bars last for over half an hour) and it must be the only movement in symphonic music that calls for a hammer among the percussion instruments.

In the *Seventh Symphony* (1905), as in the Third, Mahler gives vent to his love of Nature, only on a much more exalted plane. As well as being a complete contrast to the pessimism of its predecessor, the Seventh is perhaps the most positive of Mahler's symphonies. Among its more striking features are the guitar and mandoline in the fourth movement, a Serenade marked "Andante amoroso."

The colossal *Eighth Symphony* was to all intents and purposes completed at Maiernigg in 1906, though the finishing touches to the scoring were not applied until after Mahler had shaken the dust of Vienna from his feet the following year. It is on an immense scale and requires eight soloists—three sopranos, two altos, a tenor, a baritone and a bass—as well as a boys' choir, two mixed choirs, organ, and full orchestra, the kind of forces that Berlioz loved to deploy. The symphony consists of two ap-

Richard Strauss

Richard Wagner

parently incompatible settings, first of the ancient Christian Whitsuntide hymn "Veni Creator Spiritus", and afterwards of the closing scene of Part II of Goethe's "Faust", with a "chorus mysticus" to intone the final stanza "Alles Vergängliche ist nur ein Gleichnis".

The "slings and arrows of outrageous fortune" that assailed Mahler after the Eighth Symphony—the death of his daughter, the break with the Vienna Opera, and the shock of the doctor's diagnosis—inevitably had their effect on the composer's last two masterpieces. *Das Lied von der Erde* (1908), a "symphony for full orchestra with tenor and alto (or baritone) voices" is a symphonic song-cycle based on a set of old Chinese poems on Man's farewell to life on earth. The word "symphonic" gives a false impression, because in fact the orchestral accompaniment is often of almost chamber-music delicacy. The last song, "Abschied", is almost unbearably poignant in view of the composer's knowledge that his own days were numbered.

The *Ninth Symphony* (1909), written at Toblach in South Tyrol, opens up quite new horizons. Man appears as no longer constrained by his own mortality: he rises above the things of this world and contemplates them from without, as it were. This explains the unusual order of the movements, the two slow movements flanking the two strongly contrasted and agitated inner movements. The first and last movements are in the nature of a farewell, charged with anguish and affection, to a world so given over to the vanity of materialism (second movement) and so bent on its own destruction (third movement) that it can never comprehend its true purpose. So the Ninth is in many ways a return to the pessimism of the Sixth, only in a state of transfiguration. In the final movement the composer reconciles himself to the certainty of impending death. "I am ready," he seems to say, "ready and not afraid."

The end came while he was working on a Tenth Symphony, though the Finale of the Ninth makes it clear that Mahler must have known he would never live to finish another symphony. Of the two completed movements, one is a wonderful, spacious Adagio that shows no falling-off whatever in his creative powers: on the contrary, it ranks with the Adagio of the Fourth and the Adagietto of the Fifth as one of his supreme achievements.

The great Austrian composers seem to have been fated never to hear their last works, and Mahler was no exception: he never lived to hear either "Das Lied von der Erde" or the Ninth Symphony, let alone the unfinished Tenth.

CHAPTER ELEVEN

The Two Richards
Richard Wagner and Richard Strauss

Nearly all the great composers, and a good many minor ones as well, visited Vienna at some time or another during their lives. It was the literally riotous success of Rossini's visit in 1822 that sparked off the first of many subsequent crises at the Vienna Opera: so cock-a-hoop was the Italian faction that Carl Maria von Weber, whose "Der Freischütz" had captivated Vienna in November 1821, had to be specially commissioned by the Vienna Opera to counter the Italian invasion with a new opera "Euryanthe" (first performance 25 October 1823). The first Vienna performance of "Der Freischütz" in the presence of the Emperor Franz must have involved some ingenious improvisation: the Emperor could not stand the noise of guns going off on the stage, so the guns had to be replaced by bows and arrows, and in the Wolf's Glen Max and Kaspar, instead of making magic bullets, pottered about looking for magic arrows in a hollow oak-tree. As for Rossini, Charles Sealsfield wrote from Vienna as late as 1828: "A new opera by Rossini attracts as much, if not more, attention as the opening of Parliament in London."

Robert Schumann was one of the few great composers for whom Vienna seems to have had few charms. He lodged at Schönlaterngasse 7a in the First District in 1838, and his Schubert researches culminated in his extracting the manuscript of the Great C major Symphony from Schubert's brother Ferdinand, a feat for which the musical world will be for ever in his debt; but on 10 October he wrote home: "I must say I should not like to live here very long. Serious-minded people and serious pursuits are neither called for nor understood. My only consolation is the environment. Yesterday, I went to the cemetery where Beethoven and Schubert are buried."

Vivaldi, Chopin, Berlioz, Liszt and Verdi all included the Austrian capital in their travels, the latter being neither the first nor the last visitor to Vienna to complain of the "infernal wind". Verdi conducted "Nabucco" in 1843 and returned to Vienna in 1875 to conduct two performances of "Aida" and four of his new Requiem, after which he was awarded the order of Franz Joseph and received in audience by the Emperor (after all, Verdi was an Austrian subject by birth). None of these "non-residents" however made such a lasting impact on Vienna in general, and the Vienna Opera in particular, as the two Richards, Wagner and Strauss; and although this book has no intention of adding to the already voluminous literature on the Vienna Opera, no chronicle of Viennese music would be complete without some account of how much these two composers contributed to it.

Vienna felt the full impact of Wagner (1813–1883) on a number of occasions, his first visit being in 1832 with a Symphony in C which was performed (once) in Prague the same year and was repeated fifty years later in Venice, Wagner himself conducting. At the impressionable age of nineteen he was enthusiastically responsive to Johann Strauss I, whose waltzes he found "more potent than alcohol". Though he did not stay long he ran true to form by running up substantial debts, which is perhaps why it was another sixteen years before he ventured to show his face in conservative Vienna after being involved in the revolutionary movements of 1848 to the extent of having made the acquaintance of the anarchist Michael Bakunin in Leipzig and being on the run with a Saxon warrant out against him.

The purpose of his third visit to Vienna was to supervise the dress rehearsal of "Lohengrin" (11 May 1861). Wagner's relations with the Vienna Opera alternated unpredictably between euphoria and exasperation, but on this occasion things could not have gone better. "The orchestra, singers, chorus—all were superb, unbelievably fine. The Opera here is absolutely heavenly, any number of glorious voices" he wrote. And he was given such an ovation that "I began to be afraid the applause would literally bring the house down". Still in the same mood of euphoria Wagner resolved to follow up "Lohengrin" with "Tristan and Isolde", but after seventy-seven rehearsals it was abandoned as "unplayable", and it was another twenty years before it was first performed in Vienna after Wagner's death.

Wagner's longest and most spectacular stay in Vienna was during the 1863/64 season, shortly after celebrating his fiftieth birthday. On arrival, he characteristically saw fit to issue a twenty-page tract on how opera should be organised in Vienna: being financed by the Court, the Imperial Opera should stage only German operas (presumably his own), and French and Italian opera should be left to French and Italian companies playing at privately financed theatres (what was to be done about Mozart was not quite clear). Having delivered himself of this pronouncement Wagner allowed himself a concert tour of Russia, and with the proceeds rented a villa at Hadikgasse 72 in Vienna where he worked on "Die Meistersinger" and roped in Brahms for copying parts. Even for Wagner it was a fantastic menage. The walls were festooned with silk, and the salon was dimly lit by a single lamp hanging from the ceiling. The whole of the floor was covered by heavy and unusually soft carpets into which the unwary visitor's feet sank almost up to the ankles. The working room was upholstered in lilac, with lilac hangings and bands of red and gold on the corners. For the drawing-room a rosebud pattern was considered appropriate. The curtains were of brown wool with a Persian pattern, and the armchairs were of dark red plush. The maid had to wear pink knee-breeches and be exquisitely perfumed (all this of course was before his second wife Cosima took charge of him). By March 1864 however Wagner was obliged, not for the first time in his life, to do a "moonlight flit" to escape the clutches of his creditors. "Unless a miracle happens", he wrote in his diary, "this is the end." Of course the miracle did happen in the person of King Ludwig II of Bavaria, but that is another story. Wagner's companion in this colourful episode was a certain Friederike Mayer, a sister of the Luise Dustmann who was earmarked for Isolde in the projected Vienna production of "Tristan und Isolde". As time went on however tongues began to wag, and sensing that "Tristan" might be in jeopardy Wagner packed Friederike off to Venice and never set eyes on her again.

It was not until 1872 that Wagner deemed it safe to return to Vienna, now sporting a facial growth that gave him a curious gnome-like appearance. The purpose of his visit was to conduct concerts (including the "Eroica" symphony) in the new Musikverein to raise funds for the building of his Festival Theatre at Bayreuth. While in Vienna he attended, but did not conduct, a performance of his early opera "Rienzi", which was the Emperor Franz Joseph's favourite opera and was always trotted out for the entertainment of visiting potentates. At the very first bar of the Overture Wagner stormed out of his box cursing the trumpet-player and stumped off to the buffet, where he cooled down over ice-cream before returning to his box. In the interval he sent for the Director and his staff and proceeded to give them a thorough dressing-down about the scenery, which was the Emperor's particular pride and joy. The reason for Wagner's irritation was a dispute that went right back to the 1860s, when Wagner sold Vienna the rights of "Lo-

hengrin", "The Flying Dutchman", and "Tannhäuser" for a
lump sum; but what induced him to pick on the wretched
Director instead of submitting his claim for royalties to the
appropriate Court authorities Wagner alone knew.

By the spring of 1875, when Wagner returned to Vienna
to conduct some more concerts for Bayreuth, the dispute
had still not been settled, but there had been a change of
Director at the Opera, and the new Director was well
aware of the advisability of making peace with Wagner,
particulary in view of the sensational success of his concerts
at the Musikverein. And this time Wagner had the whip-
hand: unless the royalties dispute were settled forthwith he
refused to let Vienna have the Paris version of
"Tannhäuser". The new Director at last succeeded in extracting a decision from the Court authorities whereby
Wagner was to receive back-payments on past performances, and 7 per cent performing rights henceforth. Those
in the know in Vienna were very well aware that the "emi-
nence grise" behind the whole sordid squabble was
Wagner's wife Cosima, which was why they referred to the
agreement as the "Lex Cosima". At once Wagner's euphoria returned and the Vienna Opera was the apple of his
eye: he installed himself in the Imperial Hotel, was the
guest of honour at a reception in the Opera House on
7 November, started rehearsals for "Tannhäuser" on
10 November, and on 23 November attended the premiere
conducted by Hans Richter. He also supervised the production of "Lohengrin" on 15 December, Richter again conducting. At both performances the critics were a good deal
less enthusastic than the audiences: after "Lohengrin" for
instance the redoubtable Eduard Hanslick wrote that he felt
as if he had been pole-axed.

Wagner's last appearance in Vienna was a flying visit
early in March 1876 to conduct "Lohengrin" for the first
and only time in Vienna. By now however his mood had

veered once again, his grievance this time being that he had not been invited to the turbulent Vienna premiere of "Die Meistersinger" on 27 February 1870 shortly after he and Cosima were married at Lucerne. Wagner left Vienna after only two days, vowing never to set foot in the place again. The exasperation finally triumphed over the euphoria.

In 1917, i.e. in the darkest days of the First World War, the Austrian writer Hugo von Hofmannsthal who supplied the libretti for so many of Richard Strauss's operas wrote: "This Europe of ours, in the new form it aspires to, needs a country like Austria, an essentially elastic structure, an organism permeated by an inner faith in its own being without which no cohesion between vital forces is possible. The expression 'Central Europe' is a commonplace, but for Europe, if there is to be a Europe at all, Austria is indispensable on the loftier plane of the things of the mind, especially if decisions affecting a thousand years of history are to be taken."

Prophetic words: the Dual Monarchy disintegrated the following year and "Austria", i.e. all that was left after the Succession States had helped themselves to as much as they reckoned they could get away with, became a small Republic of some seven million souls, nearly a quarter of whom lived in Vienna. One of the last acts of the Court Intendant in charge of the Imperial Opera was to sound the Bavarian composer Richard Strauss (1864–1949), like Hofmannsthal one of the founders of the Salzburg Festival, on whether he would be prepared to take up an appointment as Director of the Vienna Opera, following the spectacular success of some performances he had conducted during a "Strauss Week" the previous spring. A few weeks later the Monarchy was a thing of the past and the Imperial Opera eventually became the State Opera, but in spite of the pitiful conditions in the stricken capital—no work, no fuel, no food—the first Republican Government decided that the Opera was not an expensive luxury but a national necessity, the same decision as the Second Republic was to take in similar conditions after the Second World War. That the State Opera kept its head above water was due almost entirely to its first post-war Director Franz Schalk; and Richard Strauss was duly offered a post as Co-Director with Schalk, his contract stipulating that he was to be at Vienna's disposal for five consecutive months every year and conduct forty performances. By accepting, Strauss demonstrated his support of the ideals Hofmannsthal had proclaimed the year before, as well as his own belief in the future of Austria, though few would have given much for the new Republic's chances of survival in those first precarious post-war years. Yet 1919 was the Opera's most brilliant year since the legendary Mahler era, culminating in the world premiere of "Die Frau ohne Schatten" on 10 October, Schalk conducting. This was the first and last time Vienna was accorded the honour of the world premiere of an opera by Richard Strauss. The first performance was not an unqualified success, and it is perhaps the complexity of Hofmannsthal's libretto that has been mainly responsible for "the Frau's" very slow headway in the Anglo-Saxon world: it was not until 1966 for instance that she eventually reached the New York "Met".

The Strauss-Hofmannsthal collaboration that had begun with the shattering impact of "Elektra" in 1909 was continued with "Der Rosenkavalier" in 1911, and on 4 October 1916 the revised "Vienna" version of "Ariadne auf Naxos" was given its world premiere in Vienna with a cast including Maria Jeritza *and* Lotte Lehmann.

No doubt Strauss had his reasons for allotting the world premiere of "Der Rosenkavalier", the most Viennese opera ever written, to Dresden instead of Vienna, but Vienna enjoyed it within a week or two of its premiere, on 8 April 1911 to be precise, the production being supervised, albeit anonymously, by Max Reinhardt. The correspondence between Strauss and Hofmannsthal has enabled posterity to follow the evolution of this miraculous work at every step. The idea first came to Hofmannsthal shortly after "Elektra", and Strauss was set on writing a "Mozart" opera. The result is a "comedy for music" set in the Vienna of Maria Theresia's day (1740–1780) with a libretto written in a kind of "Maria Theresia" Austrian dialect freely larded with French, a language that never was. Despite its subtitle, "Der Rosenkavalier" must be the only opera that can be (and indeed has been, at the Schloss Theater at Schönbrunn and in the Theater in der Josefstadt) performed as a straight play without music. The Press notices of the Vienna premiere make hilarious reading today: "A farce which in places degenerates to the level of operetta—an intruder from the nethermost regions of operetta—it will enjoy as brief a homunculus existence as other pieces with an appeal that depends solely on their curiosity value—Strauss is one of those people who raise their voices loudest when they have least to say—a Field Marshal's wife indulging in erotic diversions well after reaching the age of retirement—the music is excessively morbid and unnatural, a hullaballoo that is enough to dissolve the marrow of one's bones—Ochs is just a dunghill Falstaff, a Don Juan out of a cesspool." And so on. These gems surely bear out the truth of Jan Sibelius's comforting words to a young composer who was complaining about being unfairly mauled by the critics: "Young man, always remember that nobody has ever put up a statue to a critic."

Towards the end of his five years as Co-Director of the Vienna Opera Strauss presented the Austrian National Library with the original manuscript of the full score of "Der Rosenkavalier", and in return was given a plot of land on which to build himself a villa (Jacquingasse 8, Third District).

During his terms as Co-Director Strauss was increasingly in favour of consolidating the classical repertoire instead of giving up-and-coming local talent a chance. Rightly or wrongly, he held that the Vienna Opera was not the place, and the 1920s were not the time, for experiments. His attitude to contemporary composers was far from objective, and he even dismissed Mahler, who had done so much for him in his early days, as "a good conductor but not really a composer at all". Nothing is more typical of Strauss's attitude to composition and fellow-composers than a brief encounter with Hans Pfitzner at the premiere of Pfitzner's opera "Palestrina" in Munich. "Just imagine", said Pfitzner, "this opera has cost me ten years' unremitting toil." Strauss looked puzzled, and after Pfitzner had gone on his way he muttered to a friend who had heard the conversation: "I can't understand why the fellow goes on composing if he finds it so difficult."

In administrative matters too the friction between Strauss and Schalk became increasingly embarrassing: Schalk felt that he was being treated little better than a stooge, and that Strauss was running the Vienna Opera as if it were his own personal Bayreuth. "There's one thing about our Opera Director Strauss, he certainly makes no bones about Strauss being his favourite composer" was how some sections of the community saw the situation, and the pro-Schalk faction began to sharpen their knives. In the end it was over a trivial administrative matter in November 1934 that Strauss was manoeuvred into an untenable situation when he was not even in Vienna, but away in Dresden supervising the preparations for the first performance of "Intermezzo". Angry and humiliated, Strauss severed his connection with the Vienna Opera an hour or two before the premiere of "Intermezzo". Schalk was left in sole charge, and it was two years before the rift was healed and Strauss conducted a performance of "Elektra" at the Vienna Opera in December 1926. He was also present at the first Vienna performance of another of his operas with a pronounced Viennese flavour, "Arabella", in October 1933.

During the Second World War he continued to pay frequent visits to Vienna, but usually as an artistic adviser and not as a conductor, supervising for instance the first Vienna performance of "Daphne" in 1940. The last performance he conducted at the Vienna Opera was "Salome" in 1942, and the climax of his long association with Vienna were the celebrations, under the auspices of the Third Reich, of his eightieth birthday in 1944, in the course of which he supervised, but did not conduct, a number of his own operas. And at eighty-five he was still composing with the same professional craftsmanship and facility as he had shown at the age of seventeen. Perhaps we had better leave it at that.

CHAPTER TWELVE

Three Viennese Institutions
The Vienna Philharmonic Orchestra—The Gesellschaft der Musikfreunde—The Vienna Boys' Choir

If Vienna really is the city of unlimited improbabilities, by no means the least extraordinary of them is the *Vienna Philharmonic Orchestra*, a body that is self-administrative, hardly gives evening concerts in Vienna, and has two distinct functions and titles but no permanent conductor.

The first "Philharmonic" concert, conducted by Otto Nicolai, took place in the Redoutensaal of the Hofburg at 12.30 p.m. on Easter Monday 28 March 1842, and the experiment was repeated on 28 November of the same year. At his third concert on 19 March 1843 Nicolai conducted Beethoven's Ninth Symphony, for which, as he recorded in his diary, he allowed himself the luxury of thirteen rehearsals. Later, Nicolai himself admitted that the founding of the "Philharmonic" concerts was his most important contribution to the musical life of Vienna, not excluding his opera "The Merry Wives of Windsor".

One of the first to express his admiration of the Philharmonic tradition established by Nicolai was Hector Berlioz. "The orchestra that Nicolai has personally built up and trained under his baton", Berlioz wrote to his friend Humbert Ferrand in 1845, "may have its equal, but it certainly has no superior. Quite apart from its precision, its temperament and its outstanding technical skill, it produces a wonderful purity of tone which is doubtless due to the meticulous accuracy of the instrumental tuning and to the strict avoidance of slipshod intonation . . ."

A milestone in the history of the Vienna Philharmonic Orchestra was the arrival of Gustav Mahler as Director of the Imperial Opera: in 1898 he also took over the Philharmonic concerts, and it was under his baton that the orchestra ventured on its first foreign tour, to the World Exhibition in Paris. The visit was accorded Imperial recognition and culminated in the award of the Golden Wreath of Honour from the hands of Camille Saint-Saens, President of the Exhibition's Music Committee. The Mahler tradition was carried on by Bruno Walter, who conducted the orchestra for the first time in 1907, and for the last time on 29 May 1960.

In 1903 the Philharmonic decided to reverse the policy of having a permanent conductor and invited some of the most illustrious conductors of the day to conduct one or two concerts a year. The orchestra established a particularly cordial relationship with Richard Strauss, who conducted it on no fewer than eighty-five occasions. From his sixtieth birthday until his death in 1949 the orchestra lost no opportunity of honouring him whenever an occasion presented itself, while Strauss in return wrote a number of works specially for the Vienna Philharmonic.

In 1908 the orchestra reverted to the "permanent conductor" system and appointed Felix von Weingartner, who held the post for the next nineteen years. It was Weingartner who in 1917, in view of the immense popularity of the Philharmonic concerts, introduced the practice of holding a public final rehearsal on the Saturday afternoon preceding the actual concert on Sunday morning. In 1922 he also took the orchestra to South America, its first overseas tour. When Weingartner departed to Basle in 1927 Wilhelm Furtwängler was invited to succeed him, and so began an intimate association that was only ended by Furtwängler's untimely death.

In addition to being a concert-giving organisation the

Vienna Philharmonic Orchestra is also the Vienna State Opera Orchestra, the permanent orchestra of the Vienna Opera, and this is why its concerts are seldom given in the evenings, but at 11 a.m. on Sundays. The concerts are not publicly advertised and admission is theoretically restricted to subscribers, though it is usually possible to pick up a "return" a day or two beforehand. Subscribers' tickets are cherished heirlooms and hardly ever come on the market, while the concerts are social occasions of the first magnitude. It follows that a Philharmonic audience is on the conservative side, and the orchestra does not feel itself bound to experiment with more than the barest minimum of contemporary music: its policy is to cherish and preserve for posterity the Viennese classical tradition.

Despite the orchestra's dual function, foreign tours are embarked upon from time to time, particularly when its duties at the State Opera are taken over by a visiting company. In October/November 1959 the orchestra actually went round the world in forty days with Herbert von Karajan, the route being India, Thailand, the Philippines, Hong Kong, Japan, Hawaii, and the United States. Twenty-six concerts were given in seventeen different cities, including a Johann Strauss concert in Tokyo conducted by the leader, Willy Boskovsky.

During a tour of South America with Richard Strauss in 1923 the Chairman of the orchestra remarked: "We are the successors of artists who learned their craft from Beethoven. It was with the sound of our orchestra in mind that Brahms and Bruckner wrote their symphonies. We have been given guidance and instruction by great composers, and we know that it is the wonderful city we live in that endows us with our strength and quality." And Wilhelm Furtwängler's speech at the centenary celebrations of 1942 included some words that could hardly have been better chosen: "In my view, the chief reason for this orchestra's unique position in European music is that it is an out-and-out Viennese orchestra. With very few exceptions, all its members were born and bred in Vienna. The whole of this composite body of musicians, of first-class virtuoso performers are sons of the same countryside, the same environment. This is something you will not find anywhere else in the world."

What makes the *Gesellschaft der Musikfreunde,* founded in 1812, such an unique feature of Viennese musical life is that although it is the largest and most venerable concert-giving organisation in the world, it is the only body of its kind that owns concert-halls and offices (the Musikverein) but has no orchestra of its own. Instead, every year some half dozen of the world's finest orchestras are invited to come to Vienna and show what they can do, and the Vienna Symphony Orchestra shares the season's programmes to the tune of a dozen or so symphony concerts a year.

The present Musikverein building is a product of the "Gründerzeit", the great expansion of Vienna during the 1860's and 1870's. Details of a grandiose plan for the modernisation of medieval Vienna were set out in an Imperial Edict of 20 December 1857: the walls and bastions were to be razed, and the glacis was to make way for a splendid thoroughfare enclosing the city on three sides. By a further Imperial decree of 27 February 1863 the Gesellschaft der Musikfreunde was granted a plot of land between this new "Ringstrasse" and the river Wien. A design for a new "Musikverein" building was submitted by the Danish architect Theophil Hansen: work started on it on 17 June 1867, and the Society moved in on 31 December 1869. The programme of its first concert in the Main Hall on 6 January 1870 was a bizarre jumble of choral and orchestral excerpts from the works of J. S. Bach, Haydn, Mozart, Beethoven

The Theater an der Wien in the 19th century

The Vienna Opera in the summer of 1945

and Schubert; but the smaller hall (now the Brahms Saal) opened on 19 January 1870 with a piano recital by no less a personage than Clara Schumann. From 1872–1875 the Society's symphony concerts were conducted by Brahms, the programmes including the first Vienna performance of Handel's "Saul", Brahms's own "Song of Destiny" and "Alto Rhapsody", Berlioz' "Harold in Italy", and J. S. Bach's "St Matthew Passion".

In the last days of the Second World War a Russian shell went through the Main Hall's superb coffer-ceiling, and the building lost all its windows during the street fighting before the Russian forces finally controlled the city. The damage was repaired in a matter of months, and the Main Hall re-opened at 11 a.m. on 16 September 1945 with a concert by the Vienna Philharmonic Orchestra conducted by Josef Krips, the programme consisting of Schubert's "Unfinished" and Bruckner's Seventh Symphony, both of which struck exactly the right note. Other memorable concerts were the occasion of Wilhelm Furtwängler's first post-war appearance in Vienna on 8 September 1947 (Mendelssohn's "Midsummer Night's Dream" Overture and Violin Concerto, and Beethoven's Third Symphony) and Bruno Walter's last concert with the Vienna Philharmonic on 29 May 1960 (the "Unfinished" and Mahler's Fourth).

The Main Hall of the Vienna Musikverein can claim to be the most splendid concert hall in the world, the appeal to the eye being surpassed only by the appeal to the ear, i.e. the perfection of the acoustics. It has been said that the walls of the Main Hall seem actually to vibrate in sympathy with the Philharmonic's strings. But a price has had to be paid for these unique acoustics: in order to preserve them, the building was placed under the Austrian equivalent of the National Trust, which means that any structural alterations that could possibly affect the acoustics are ruled out. In other words, no air-conditioning.

As well as being Vienna's principal concert-giving association, the Gesellschaft der Musikfreunde is also the landlord of the whole Musikverein building, which also houses the famous piano firm of Bösendorfer and the offices of the Vienna Philharmonic Orchestra, which hires the Main Hall for its own independent series of subscription concerts.

The archives, library and museum on the top floor of the Musikverein contain over fifty thousand works, including some priceless treasures of inestimable value that the Society's founders can never have dreamed of: the original manuscripts, for instance, of all Schubert's symphonies except the Fifth, and of Beethoven's Third Symphony with the composer's famous and furious deletion of the dedication to Napoleon. Among other Schubert exhibits are fragments of the manuscript of the song "Der Tod und das Mädchen", relics of the weird action of Schubert's half-brother Andreas who as a schoolmaster's son showed his reverence for scholarship by snipping the manuscript into pieces and distributing them among his friends: the Gesellschaft der Musikfreunde has recovered and pieced together six of the fragments. A visit to the library can also indulge in the moving experience of opening a box containing no fewer than 135 of Beethoven's letters. Perhaps the library's most important collective acquisition was due to the generosity of Johannes Brahms, who bequeathed to the Society his entire collection of manuscripts, including that of Mozart's G minor Symphony.

The collection of old instruments is housed not in the Musikverein but in the Music Department of the Kunsthistorisches Museum, to which it is officially "on loan". The collection includes exotic instruments from such improbable sources as Indian villages in the United States and negro kraals in Africa.

Unlike Vienna's other concert-giving organisation, the Konzerthaus on the other side of the river Wien, the Gesellschaft der Musikfreunde rarely indulges in experiments with ultra-modern music, nor do its members and subscribers expect it to. But this is not to say that it turns a deaf ear to twentieth-century music: a perusal of its programmes of no fewer than eight different series of subscription concerts a year will show that today as always it still aspires to live up to its aim of preserving the Austrian classical tradition and giving music by contemporary Austrian composers a fair hearing.

"Alle guten Dinge sind drei" says an Austrian proverb: "all good things come in threes". And our third Viennese institution, the *Vienna Boys' Choir* (Wiener Sängerknaben), is certainly a "good thing". It was originally constituted by Maximilian I in June 1498 to "supply music for the Mass", and this is exactly what it still does today in the Hofburg Chapel at 9.25 every Sunday morning from 15 September to 30 June, the tenors and basses being provided by the Vienna Opera and the orchestra by a section of the Vienna Philharmonic. In the Hofburg Chapel the Masses of Mozart, Haydn, Schubert and Bruckner, not to mention Beethoven's wonderful Mass in C Op 86, can be heard as they were originally meant to be sung, i.e. liturgically.

The Vienna Boys' Choir is so well-known all over the western world that little remains to be added in this context except to congratulate the appropriate authorities on ensuring that it survived the cataclysmic aftermaths of two World Wars and is still going strong. The choir all but went under in 1919—only fifteen boys stuck out the appalling post-war conditions in Vienna—but in 1924 it was reformed by Rektor Josef Schmitt, since when it has consolidated its existence with the help of the profits from its world-wide tours (except of course during the grisly interlude between 1938 and 1945). In point of fact there are four choirs, not one, and with such ample resources it is a relatively simple matter to ensure that a least one of the choirs is available for foreign tours all the year round. One strikingly successful chapter in the Vienna Boys' Choir's history was a tour of the United States in the course of which it featured in a Walt Disney film which there is no need to specify further. Its programmes on tour generally open with examples of 16th century polyphonic church music (Palestrina, Lassus, etc.). Part II will consist of a play or opera in period costume to music by Haydn, Mozart or Schubert, followed by folk-songs and choral versions of Viennese waltzes.

In conclusion, it may perhaps be permissible to return to that overworked word "unique" and paraphrase George Orwell by asserting that whereas all three of these Viennese institutions are unique, the Hofburg Chapel is the most unique of the three: liturgical Masses sung by a choir and soloists and accompanied by a sizable orchestra can only be heard in Austria.

CHAPTER THIRTEEN

Opera in Vienna

Although this book has emphatically disclaimed any intention of swelling the spate of literature on the Vienna Opera, it is impossible (in the words of a character in a play by the Viennese actor-playwright Johann Nestroy) to "not even ignore it". There it stands at the city's busiest centre, Vienna's most prominent landmark after St Stephen's Cathedral, and what goes on within its massive walls is frequently front page news.

Like the Musikverein, the Opera House is a product of the expansion of Vienna decreed by Franz Joseph I in 1857. In the selection of a site the new Opera House was given pride of place, being allotted ground at the intersection of the grand new Ringstrasse and the main road to Trieste. But the ceremonial opening fell distinctly flat: not for the first time the ingrained Viennese mistrust of anything new asserted itself. The diehards were against the new house from the start (what was wrong with the historic Kärntnertor Theater anyway?), while even those who recognized the necessity for a more commodious house stood aghast at what they were now being asked to patronise, a "massive monstrosity" that looked like "a bogged-down packing-case" because there were no steps leading up to it. So malicious was some of the criticism that one of the architects of the new house took his life, and the other died of shock two months later. Neither lived to attend the ceremonial opening on 25 May 1869. But as time went on the Viennese not only became reconciled to their new Opera House but even came to regard it as their pride and joy, one excitable enthusiast even describing it as "a splendid illustration of the old saying that architecture is music in stone", which is perhaps going a bit too far.

Opera in Vienna was originally a product of the baroque era, an entertainment for the Imperial family. After one or two desultory experiments dating back to as early as 1625, the first to introduce a "dramma per musica" to Vienna at regular intervals, as part of her dowry so to speak, was Eleonora Gonzaga of Mantua, the third wife of Ferdinand III (1637–1657), himself a competent composer. These early baroque operas were performed in one of the ballrooms of the Hofburg, probably on the site of the present Redouten Säle. Later, the Vienna Court was in contact with the great Venetian composer Claudio Monteverdi and his successors Francesco Cavalli and Marco Antonio Cesti, who was Deputy Kapellmeister to Leopold I for three years (1666–1669). It was under Leopold I (1657–1705), himself a composer, conductor and actor all in one, that baroque opera came to its full flowering in Vienna in the form of lavish popular festivities open to all and sundry; and by the reign of Maria Theresia (1740–1780) opera was no longer the exclusive prerogative of the aristocracy. In 1741 she handed over the disused "Hofballhaus" near what is now the Michaelerplatz to an actor-impresario named Carl Selliers, on condition that he "should convert the interior at his own expense into a theatre for operas and plays, with accommodation, propriis sumtibus, for an orchestra and an audience, including galleries but no boxes except two for the Imperial household; and that he should therein provide, for the diversion of the public and Her Majesty, a play or opera in either German or Italian every evening as the Court should require; further that the said Selliers should be permitted to charge each member of the audience, except the occupants of the Imperial boxes, a sum appropriate to the position of his seat". This theatre, which eventually be-

Heute Freytag den 30ten September 1791.

Werden die Schauspieler in dem kaiserl. königl. privil. Theater auf der
Wieden die Ehre haben aufzuführen

Zum Erstenmale:

Die

Zauberflöte.

Eine grosse Oper in 2 Akten, von Emanuel Schikaneder.

Personen

Sarastro.	.	.	.	Hr. Gerl.
Tamino.	.	.	.	Hr. Schack.
Sprecher.	.	.	.	Hr. Winter.
Erster)	.	.	.	Hr. Schikaneder der ältere.
Zweiter) Priester.	.	.	.	Hr. Kistler.
Dritter)	.	.	.	Hr. Moll.
Königin der Nacht.	.	.	.	Mad. Hofer.
Pamina ihre Tochter.	.	.	.	Mlle. Gottlieb.
Erste)	.	.	.	Mlle. Klöpfer.
Zweite) Dame.	.	.	.	Mlle. Hofmann.
Dritte)	.	.	.	Mad. Schack.
Papageno.	.	.	.	Hr. Schikaneder der jüngere.
Ein altes Weib.	.	.	.	Mad. Gerl.
Monostatos ein Mohr.	.	.	.	Hr. Nouseul.
Erster)	.	.	.	Hr. Gieseke.
Zweiter) Sklav.	.	.	.	Hr. Frasel.
Dritter)	.	.	.	Hr. Starke.
Priester, Sklaven, Gefolge.				

Die Musik ist von Herrn Wolfgang Amade Mozart, Kapellmeister, und wirklicher
K. K. Kammerkompositeur. Herr Mozard wird aus Hochachtung für ein gnädi-
ges und verehrungswürdiges Publikum, und aus Freundschaft gegen den Verfas-
ser des Stücks, das Orchester heute selbst dirigiren.

Die Bücher von der Oper, die mit zwei Kupferstichen versehen sind, wo Herr Schikaneder in der Rolle als Papageno nach wahrem Kostüm gestochen ist, werden bei der
Theater-Kassa vor 30 kr. verkauft.

Herr Gayl Theatermahler und Herr Nessthaler als Dekorateur schmeicheln sich nach den vorgeschriebe-
nen Plan des Gedicht, mit möglichster Künstlichkeit gearbeitet zu haben.

Die Eintrittspreise sind wie gewöhnlich.

Der Anfang ist um 7 Uhr.

*Playbill of the first night on September 30,
1791 in Vienna*

came the Burgtheater, was connected with the Palace by a private corridor, but its real significance lay in its also being open to the ordinary citizens. It was at this theatre that Christoph Willibald Gluck, who was appointed Court Kapellmeister in 1760, staged his first "reformed" operas ("Orfeo ed Euridice" 1762), and it was here too that Mozart's "Die Entführung", "Figaro" and "Così fan tutte" were first performed.

A name which keeps cropping up in the annals of Viennese music is the Theater an der Wien. If the Schloss Theater at Schönbrunn is Vienna's oldest surviving theatre still in use, the Theater an der Wien can point to an illustrious, if somewhat chequered history that no other theatre in Vienna can rival. It opened in 1801 as an ancillary stage to the highly successful theatre (long since demolished) on the opposite side of the river Wien that had assured itself of immortality by staging the first performance of "Die Zauberflöte" in the autumn of 1791. Both these theatres were run by the actor-impresario Emanuel Schikaneder, who created the part of Papageno, as is commemorated by the group of figures above the "Papageno" door at the Theater an der Wien's side entrance, a door through which Beethoven, Schubert and Johann Strauss all passed at one time or another. Schikaneder was an extremely astute if somewhat unprincipled character who had no intention of hiding his light under a bushel, and on the playbills announcing Mozart's "Die Zauberflöte" he took good care that his name was billed in very much larger letters than Mozart's. He could at any rate boast that his new "Theater an der Wien" was the largest theatre in Vienna, a particularly striking feature being the depth of the stage, which was why from time to time the theatre was even used for tournaments. In 1804 Schikaneder's association with the Theater an der Wien came to an end in distinctly shady circumstances, and the new management decided to offer more solid, though less varied and spectacular, fare than Schikaneder had served up. In 1805 Beethoven actually lived in the theatre while preparing his "Leonora", (the first version of "Fidelio"), which was first performed there on 20 December 1805.

In 1810 the Court acquired the Kärntnertor Theater which became officially known as the "Imperial and Royal Opera House by the Kärntnertor" on the site occupied by the present Hotel Sacher. From now on the domains of the two Court theatres were clearly defined: drama at the Burgtheater and music at the Kärntnertor Theater, which thereby became the headquarters of opera in Vienna until the opening of the new Opera House on the Ringstrasse in 1869. The Theater an der Wien, on the other hand, went over to lighter fare, and its very existence became increasingly precarious.

The Kärntnertor Theater had at its disposal two ensembles, one Italian and the other German, and was later leased to an Italian impresario who saw to it that the Italian faction, well catered for by Rossini, eventually came out on top, despite the sensational success of Weber's "Der Freischütz" in 1821. The Italian victory was inevitable: Italian opera was the product of a style and routine that had been perfected over a considerable period of time, whereas German-language opera was still in its embryo stage and apart from one or two isolated masterpieces lacked any consistent and established style. Even Weber's "Euryanthe", written specially for the Kärntnertor Theater, could not stand up to Rossini and Gaetano Donizetti, later reinforced by the new star in the ascendant, Giuseppe Verdi, whose Vienna performance of "Nabucco" on 4 April 1853 was the first time a Verdi opera had ever been performed outside Italy.

The revolutions of 1848 however sent the Italians packing, for the time being at any rate, and German-language operas such as Friedrich von Flotow's "Martha" and Otto Nicolai's "Merry Wives of Windsor" became the order of the day in Vienna. By the 1860s however it was becoming increasingly obvious that the Kärntnertor Theater, for all its venerable tradition, was far too cramped and ill-equipped to cope with the new dimensions required by Richard Wagner, for instance, and it finally closed its doors on 17 April 1870, almost a year after the opening of the new Opera House on the Ringstrasse. During these eleven months the remaining operas in the repertoire were gradually transferred one by one from the old house to the new, so that for almost a whole year performances were actually being given on alternate nights at two opera houses within about a hundred yards of each other! The war between the Italian and the German factions came to an end and was succeeded by the interminable conflict between the Wagnerites and the anti-Wagnerites, between reaction and revolution. The first Wagner performance at the Imperial Opera was "Lohengrin" in 1858.

By the turn of the century Mahler was carrying out his drastic reforms, which included at long last a proper balance between Italian and German-language operas. It was also under Mahler's aegis that singers of the calibre of Leo Slezak and Richard Mayr made their bow in Vienna, the former being gifted with a lively and infectious sense of humour that was brilliantly deployed in parts such as Alfred in "Die Fledermaus", and the latter being assured of immortality as the creator of the role of Baron Ochs in "Der Rosenkavalier".

During the First World War Vienna enjoyed its first performance of Richard Strauss's "Ariadne auf Naxos" with the positively awesome combination of Maria Jeritza and Lotte Lehmann in the same cast. The mercurial and captivating Maria Jeritza was also Vienna's first Tosca after making her sensational Vienna debut in 1908 in

Puccini's "Manon Lescaut" at Vienna's second opera house, the Volksoper, which now specialises in Viennese operetta, light opera in German, and American musicals. In Toscanini's view Lotte Lehmann was the finest "Fidelio" of the century, quite apart from her superb stage presence. Another casual visitor to the Vienna Opera at this time was Enrico Caruso.

With the disintegration of the Monarchy in 1918 the Imperial Opera became the State Opera, with Franz Schalk and Richard Strauss as Co-Directors, and soon established itself as a world-power in the domain of music with the world-premiere of Strauss's "Die Frau ohne Schatten" on 10 October 1919, Schalk conducting. A later Director, Clemens Krauss, conducted the first Vienna performance of Alban Berg's "Wozzeck" as well as introducing Vienna to two outstanding tenors, Jan Kiepura and Max Lorenz, the latter a Wagner specialist. Many of the singers and conductors who captivated Vienna between the wars are still household words—Kirsten Flagstad, Lauritz Melchior, Beniamino Gigli, Richard Tauber, Bruno Walter, Wilhelm Furtwängler, Hans Knappertsbusch, and Arturo Toscanini, to name only a few.

Towards the end of the Second World War the Vienna Opera was closed down in pursuance of the policy of "total war", the last performance being appropriately enough "Götterdämmerung" on 30 June 1944. And then came the "dies irae" on 12 March 1945 when the house received several direct hits during a daylight air-raid and was soon a mass of smoking debris, only the west façade and loggia surviving. Yet although half the city was in ruins by the time the war ended a few weeks later, the rebuilding of the Vienna Opera House was rated a nationwide top priority: but where was the Opera to find a home during the work of reconstruction, which was expected to take at least ten years? Improvisation, ingenuity, and a determination that "the show must go on" found an answer, and on 1 May 1945, even before the war in Europe was over, "Le Nozze di Figaro" was being given at the Volksoper, which had come through the fighting almost unscathed. At the same time, it was decided to renovate the venerable Theater an der Wien, which during the war had suffered the indignity of being used as an army clothing-store. Despite daunting technical difficulties and perilous dilapidation, and with woefully inadequate scenery and costumes, the ten years at the Theater an der Wien can be seen in retrospect to have been among the Vienna Opera's finest hours, when the celebrated "Mozart style" was perfected by Josef Krips with an ensemble that can seldom, if ever, have been surpassed in the annals of the Vienna Opera. The move into the reconstructed house on the Ringstrasse took place on 5 November 1955, six months after the State Treaty had restored Austria's sovereignty after seventeen years of occupation. An audience of V.I.P.s from the four corners of the earth assembled in Vienna for a performance of "Fidelio" conducted by the Opera's newly-appointed Director, Karl Böhm, and a vast concourse of Viennese citizens listened on their portable radios outside in the raw November weather.

To cast invidious distinction among the many outstanding artists who have graced the Vienna Opera since the Second World War would be grossly unfair in the present context, but nobody who had the privilege of being present will forget the "Fidelio" conducted by Josef Krips on 6 October 1945 with which the Theater an der Wien reopened; or the miraculous performances of "Così fan tutte" with an ensemble of Irmgard Seefried, Elisabeth Höngen, Emmy Loose, Paul Schöffler, Anton Dermota, and Erich Kunz. Among other popular post-war favourites have been Hilde Güden, Ljuba Welitsch, Sena Jurinac and Christa Ludwig. As well as Josef Krips, the outstanding conductors have been Karl Böhm, Herbert von Karajan (who was Artistic Director 1956–1964), and the effervescent Leonard Bernstein, whose "Falstaff" remains unforgettable.

No non-Viennese can fully comprehend what the destruction of the Opera House in 1945 meant to the population as a whole, coming as it did on top of the destruction of St Stephen's Cathedral and the Burgtheater. The Opera House stood for Austria's claim to be still a world-power in the domain of music. For many Viennese, a night at the Opera is something to be looked forward to for weeks, while for tourists it is a "must", irrespective of what is on. And during the high season it is only from a resourceful hotel porter that a tourist has the slightest hope of getting a ticket at short notice.

For the last twenty years or so experts have been persistently predicting the demise of opera, which has been described as theoretically unthinkable and aesthetically downright impossible. How much longer this irrational and hideously expensive form of art can continue to survive the present upsurge in the cost of labour is anybody's guess, especially in the case of an Opera like Vienna's that is still run on repertory lines as opposed to the "stagione" system. Yet survived it has, and Gottfried von Einem's opera "Der Besuch der alten Dame" has also given the lie to the contention that since the death of Puccini the art of composing an opera that will hold its place in the repertoire is as obsolete as the genre itself. If Opera really is as moribund as they say, it is certainly dying in style.

Facts and figures may well seem inappropriate in the world of fantasy and illusion in which opera casts its spell. Suffice it to say that the Vienna State Opera has a capacity of 2,209 (567 standing after queuing for hours); but although the auditorium is relatively small compared to the immense stage, it is a good deal more comfortable than most.

There are about three hundred performances each season from 1 September to 30 June except on Christmas Eve and Good Friday, and about half a dozen new productions a season. July is the holiday month, and in August many members of the Opera play at the Salzburg Festival.

The repertoire never drops below forty operas, and in any given fortnight a dozen or so different operas can be heard, and nearly always in the original language.

By the same author

A BRIEF SURVEY OF

AUSTRIAN HISTORY

166 pages with 4 maps and 8 illustrations

Few countries can look back on such a rich, varied
and colourful history as Austria. Situated at the very
heart of Europe, Austria has been from time immemo-
rial the meeting-place of East and West. Her sphere
of interest extended from Spain to Russia and from
Italy to the Netherlands. Vienna was not only the residence of the Holy Roman Emperors, and later the
capital of the Austro-Hungarian Empire, but it was
also a European metropolis. It was from the walls of
Vienna that the Turkish onslaught on Central Europe
was rolled back in 1683, and it was in Vienna that the
Congress was held in 1814 that gave Europe peace
for almost half a century.

World War I ended in the disintegration of the
monarchy that for so many centuries had united
peoples of widely differing races and languages. All
that was left after the Treaty of St. Germain in 1919
was the remnant that is now the Republic of Austria.

Out of the ashes of 1945 Austria has again risen to
be the meeting-place between East and West, poli-
tically as well as culturally. Austria's cultural contribution is second to none, notably Baroque architecture
and in music the great classical tradition represented
by Haydn, Mozart, Beethoven, Schubert, Brahms and
Bruckner.